Agnihotra: Havan on Earth

A simple and comprehensive guide
to the practice of Agnihotra,
a Vedic fire ceremony
for personal and planetary wholeness.

"Havan"- Sanskrit word for sacred Vedic fire ceremony

Ellie Hadsall

Copyright © 2015 Ellie Hadsall
4th Edition

ALL RIGHTS RESERVED. No part of this book may be reproduced in any written, electronic, recording, or photocopying without written permission of the publisher or author. Permission in writing may be granted by the author for portions, providing reference is made to the source.

For more information on agnihotra, fire ceremony, meditation or spiritual mentoring contact: Ellie Hadsall at www.CosmicGathering.com. Free pdf printed agnihotra resources are available to download upon request.

Publisher: Cosmic Gathering

ISBN-10: 1511962941   ISBN-13: 978-1511962940

Cover Design: © 2015 Monica Hadsall

Cover and Chapter Heading Graphics: © 2011 Alex McDonell, AWM-Art, www.awm-art.com/

Photography: Easter Bonnifield, Alex McDonell, Ron Hadsall, Dooley, *Ellie Hadsall

The following slogan is copyrighted in all variations and formats including font, size, color and artistic rendering. **"Havan on Earth"**

Cover artwork and the following symbol/graphic is copyrighted in all variations and formats including size, color, shape and artistic rendering. This symbol was created to be used solely for this purpose and for this organization.

Disclaimers

Information included in this book is of an educational and general nature and should not be construed as legal or medical advice. You should consult appropriate professional sources to answer questions related to your individual situation. Exercising one's rights often entails some element of risk, and you should verify all information relevant to your situation before acting.

Although the author and publisher have made every effort to ensure that the information in this book was correct at press time, the author and publisher do not assume and hereby disclaim any liability to any party for any loss, damage, or disruption caused by errors or omissions, whether such errors or omissions result from negligence, accident, or any other cause. The author and publisher disclaim any responsibility or liability for any loss incurred as a consequence of the use of any information herein.

*Photographs in this book vary in clarity. The author's personal photos were taken over a number of years, and the quality of cameras that were used, varies. It is impossible to re-take photos of nature and scenery that no longer exit. The author has chosen to include them for interest.

Agnihotra: Havan on Earth

A simple and comprehensive guide to the practice of Agnihotra,
a Vedic fire ceremony for personal and planetary healing.

by Ellie Hadsall

It is *not* too late to help our planet.

What if *you* can help heal Mother Earth?

What if you *can* naturally support human, plant and animal life, diffuse negativity, neutralize toxins and bring spiritual, mental, emotional and physical wholeness to all life forms?

This book offers solutions for our distressed planet and her inhabitants as revealed in the ancient Vedic science of agnihotra.

This book is purposefully presented for someone who is not knowledgeable of Vedic tradition; someone who wants to participate with its benefits and do so within diverse cultural lifestyles.

This is a science and as such can be practiced by people of all cultures, spiritual traditions or religious preferences.

Knowledge and understanding gained from this book belongs to the universe.
You are encouraged to share what you learn freely with others in your own words
so that they flow through your own experience, heart and intuition.
By doing so, you and your words are empowered.
- Ellie Hadsall

Contents

1	Introduction	1
	What this book is and is not. How to use this book. Why I wrote this book for you.	
2	What is Agnihotra?	6
	Why do this ceremony. Who can perform it. Benefits. How it works. Origins. Scientific studies. Word definitions.	
3	How to Practice the Ceremony	14
	Equipment & supplies. Step-by-step, simple. Step-by-step, expanded. Agnihotra chants. Learning the chants. Translation of chants. Examples of practice.	
4	Explanation of Ceremony Components	24
	Location. Chanting the prayer. Practice of silence. Dung. Ghee. Rice. Sunrise & Sunset time.	
5	Frequently Asked Questions	28
6	Personal Agnihotra Experiences	44
7	Ash Remedies	52
	Preparing ash. Storage. Dry ash. Ash water. Quick salve. Decocted salve. Massage oil. Ash condiment. Ash for plants. Ash for animals. Ash for environment.	
8	Ghee Preparation	57
9	Dung Preparation	59
10	Build a Simple Outdoor Havan Fireplace	61
11	Resources	63
12	How to Teach Agnihotra Fire Ceremony	67
13	Simple Meditation Guidelines	71
	Preparation. Steps of meditation. Results. Helpful suggestions. What meditation does not include. Benefits of meditation. Why I meditate.	
14	My Personal Journey to Fire Ceremony	75
15	The Next Step	79
16	Observation Journal	81
	About Ellie Hadsall, Additional Books	83

AGNIHOTRA: HAVAN ON EARTH

Chapter 1

Introduction

A simple fire ceremony known as **Agnihotra** can heal Planet Earth.

Our planet and her inhabitants are moving through a metamorphosis unlike any previously known. Ancient traditions speak of this time with hope, a time to transform us into a new way of being. This is a cooperative effort. You and I are co-creators of this new world. **Agnihotra is a practice that ideally supports us in a simple yet profound way.**

Ancient Vedic science speaks of three fundamental energies supporting the Universes. First, is the energy that creates. We conceive of a belief or idea. The quantum field then accumulates necessary energy for our creation to manifest. Second, is the energy that maintains? This sustains what we created. We focus attention upon our creation, repair and re-align it; therefore it continues to exist. Third is the energy that destroys. When we outgrow a belief, expand beyond a previous idea, or are finished with what we created, we move attention away from it to something new. The old loses coherence, eventually dissolving. It loses form, releasing energy back into the quantum field to be reused and recreated into something new that is more suitable for what is needed now. Jesus the Christ knew this when he recommended "Do not put new wine into old wineskins". New is fresh, filled with vitality. Old is finished, stiff, inflexible, unable to expand.

Nature thus creates, maintains and dissolves that which is no longer useful, returning it into available energy ingredients for new life. This cycle is an essential component of existence as we know it. Dead branches and leaves compost to provide basic nutrients for micro-organisms, insects, new branches and leaves. Unlike nature, humans get attached to our creations, maintaining them long after viability has ended. We spend time and energy maintaining relationships, belongings, and commitments that have long since run their course. In doing so, we waste our vital resources. Wise ones review and release those completed creations, allowing space for re-creation to unfold. The time has arrived to let go where we have been and move into our potential. We have little choice! Current erratic weather, unpredictable natural events, unstable governments and faltering economy are signs of dissolution. Dissolution of where we have been is a sign that something new is forming and will be arriving. Ancient traditions that have remained uncorrupted by human control have long spoken of this time as a time not of despair but of hope!

Authentic ancient sciences taught that all in existence is vibrational. Modern science is re-discovering this.

Current quantum physics explains we do not consist of physical matter existing in a defined, set structure of atoms. Indeed we are an ever-flowing, miraculously adaptable field of interdimensional energy. Our energetic fields vibrate to specific frequencies. When we shift our vibration to match with confused experiences, such as fear and judgment, we misalign with our divine support frequencies, resulting in discomfort and dis-ease. Alternately, when we maintain vibrations that attune with genuineness and truth, harmony results. The vibrational field we maintain in turn affects the vibrational field of others around us.

Ancient Vedic science developed practices that "tune up" the environmental vibration frequencies to their optimum. Agnihotra (pronounced aah'-gnee-hoe'-truh) havan is one of these. In the early 1960s, enlightened havan masters spoke of a future when planetary instability would occur. They anticipated today's erratic world and taught that agnihotra would offer solutions.

Equally important to the practice of agnihotra ceremony is the practice of living in harmony with the universe. The more aligned you are with universal truth principles in your daily life, the more attuned you become with the fire. *Agnihotra's full benefits are experienced when we intentionally apply its harmonious attributes into all aspects of our lives and do not just rely upon the ceremony itself to do the work for us.* Compassion, kindness, forbearance, non-judgment, gratitude, patience, sharing with others, responsible use of personal and natural resources, being of service, respect, truthfulness, and refraining from gossip, are only a few desirable practices enumerated in spiritual traditions. By purposefully applying these, your fire practice will gather potency. In this way we expand the healing benefits of agnihotra. By offering these modes of thought and action to others we create an environment where they too can offer their best.

"Angel" agnihotra flame

It works. Yes, we can make a difference. I did not know this when I stumbled upon havan. I only knew that it was significant and I needed to participate.

What This Book Is and Is Not

In 1997 I sat in the living room of a home in Houston, Texas, attending a house blessing led by a revered Kriya Yoga saint from the Himalayas of India. As he lit fire in a small copper pyramid and began deep resonant chanting, overwhelming warmth enveloped me and unexpected tears rolled down my cheeks. Something significant was happening. I felt I was returning to a divine "knowing" I had yearned for my whole life. This was the first experience acquainting me with the loving power of Vedic fire ceremony. Already a dedicated meditator, I vowed to add this sacred fire ceremony to my life's purpose. This book is the result of that commitment.

This is a simply languaged "how to do it" book for the average person who, like me, leads a full life with daily work responsibility, family, and other commitments. It is practical and comprehensive, based on personal experience and that of my fire ceremony students. This is not intended as a scholarly work; it is intended to support you to begin your personal and planetary healing journey with fire ceremony. It is not intended to offer medical advice, which you need to obtain from a qualified professional. Rather it is presented as a simple explanation of an ancient healing science, aspects of which are being substantiated today by modern scientific research.

Currently our planet's inhabitants seek a solution to the physical, mental and emotionally toxic environment in which we dwell. The ancients offered solutions that are now coming back into the awareness of humanity. In any given age of humankind, those who are ready and willing to assist are given the necessary inspiration, knowledge, techniques, and tools. Agnihotra is one of the most treasured and potent.

I personally invite you to participate.

How to Use This Book

First, scan through the content to view the total process. As you read, questions will arise. Most answers are in this book. When reading about the process, be assured that in the following chapters you will find detailed explanation and answers to many questions. If your answer isn't here, email me at CosmicGathering@gmail.com. I will respond as soon as I can. Due to my full schedule, it may take a few days for me to respond.

Why I Wrote This Book

This is the book I wanted when learning agnihotra. It is a practical handbook, created to bring the practice of agnihotra into your life. As of this printing, the only other guidelines are on the internet, often presented with an East Indian cultural slant, or some seekers are fortunate to find a teacher. Ancient Vedic texts include mention of havan and some instruction, but it is generally not accessible or understandable to the average citizen. Since I began teaching agnihotra in 2000, many have requested this book. Most importantly, during meditating I was consistently prompted to provide it.

I invite anyone to feel welcome and capable to practice agnihotra. Although it comes from an ancient science of India known as the Vedas (Sanskrit for "knowledge" or "science"), it is not limited to that culture. This is a universal practice for any culture, race, gender or age. While I have established a personal commitment to meditate and practice healing fire ceremonies, and I appreciate East Indian culture from which many aspects of my training evolved, I am not identified by it. I respect it as I do all cultures, yet in this lifetime I dwell in the United States as a working woman, wife and mother. I live an eclectic lifestyle, practicing healing and spiritually expansive knowledge from any source that proves to be truthful, natural, practical and effective. Many sources substantiate others. For example, my current foray into the field of quantum studies supports my experience with manifesting, fire ceremony, and meditation. My life is dedicated to the practice of simple daily meditation which has been instrumental in my evolution. Fire ceremony supports this meditation practice. Together, they assist me in my life's work. For you who are curious of my personal story, a brief summary is offered in a later chapter of this book. If you skip that chapter it is okay with me. It isn't important unless it encourages you in some way.

Agnihotra at winter sunset with our teepee in the background

By 1997 I had meditated for 25 years; it was as integrated into my daily life as eating three meals, showering, and brushing my teeth. Naturally curious about life, I often pursued the "road less traveled". Yet never in my wildest dreams did I anticipate doing sacred fire ceremony. I understood it to be a spiritual practice in many cultures including Zoroastrian, Native American Indian, and East Indian, but thought of it as a religious practice from cultures far removed from my current lifestyle.

In 1997, when attending the house blessing fire ceremony, I was astonished to experience the powerful and transformative energy of this havan. After three years of searching for someone to teach me, I eventually learned the simplest fire ceremony, agnihotra, and began to practice. I am enthusiastic by nature yet also pragmatic, so I chose to prove to myself that it brought actual results. After four months of regular practice twice every day, I was astounded by the transformational results of these fires. Friends and strangers began seeking our home as a peaceful refuge, troubled neighbors resolved problems, trees destroyed from borers healed, raucous bird calls became melodious, wounded animals miraculously healed, non-blooming plants bloomed, and the list goes on and on.

I realized this was a science that could transform our neighborhood, and if multiple people practiced, transform our planet.

You can learn agnihotra from this book. You need not search three years to find a teacher. Eventually I did meet several devoted teachers who deepened my practice. Yet initially I taught myself agnihotra from a tri-fold brochure and three phone calls requesting clarification. As I experienced its benefits I began to teach it to others who experienced similar results. Once you master it in your life, I encourage you to teach it to others. Pass it on. And on. And on. Someday I anticipate seeing a neighbor light up a pyramid fire at sunrise one morning. I will ask him how he learned it, and he will say he learned it from this simple handbook, it changed his life, and he teaches it to others. I expect to know that it has come full circle. I expect to know that our planet is healing because of you.

Thanks for joining me. Together, all of us can create Havan on Earth.

A Special Note: Photographs in this book vary in clarity. Personal photos were taken over a number of years, and the quality of cameras used varies. It is impossible to re-take photos of nature and scenery that no longer exit. I have chosen to include them for interest.

- Notes -

Chapter 2

What is Agnihotra?

Agnihotra is an ancient practice wherein a fire is burned in a small copper pyramid. This simple fire ceremony is practiced for the purpose of removing harmful, negative effects so that the natural harmony of the universe can express. It isn't just a gift to our planet; it is a multi-dimensional gift to the universe.

Of all the elements mentioned in various traditions; earth, fire, wood, metal, stone, water, air and ether, the one that requires human cooperation in order to continuously express, is fire. As humans, we enjoy a special co-creative and intimate relationship with fire.

Fire is recognized as the major transforming agent in a variety of cultures across our planet. Elements that are combined and burned are changed by the fire into new chemical combinations. In the science of alchemy, fire is a fundamental agent of change. In cooking, we observe how various ingredients in a recipe affect one another. In the smithy process of making iron, the charcoal or coke, iron ore, and limestone are heated, impurities are removed, and the final transformation creates a new and stronger material, iron, that is then cast into functional forms. These are only two examples where science demonstrates that heat transforms one set of ingredients into new chemical bonds displaying new properties. Fire transforms. Fire ceremony similarly re-combines specific natural fuels, ingredients, influences of astrological events, and sound vibrations, into new energies. Depending upon the ingredients, influences of the sun, moon, heavenly bodies, and chanted sounds, the results have a specifically focused effect. These results have been repeated and proven over thousands of years.

Agni (fire) and hotra (fire pit or also one who performs a ceremonial fire) is one of the oldest of fire ceremonies. A fundamental purifying fire, its uniqueness is that it is practiced specifically at sunrise and sunset. As with all Vedic fire ceremonies, it has its own special features, purpose and results. Done with regularity, it creates an environment in which all living things receive healing, the atmosphere is purified, soil is re-enriched, and harmony reinstated.

A fire is burned in a small copper or gold pyramid. The pyramid is of precise mathematical measurement and form. This fire is performed only at sunrise or sunset. Dry cow dung is burned as the fuel. An offering of ghee (purified cow butter) mixed with grains of rice is tossed into the fire twice, while chanting a simple brief prayer in Sanskrit. Practitioner and guests sit in silence, praying, contemplating or meditating as the transformative fire continues to burn. When the flame burns out, the resulting alchemical ash is used for agricultural and healing purposes. Smoke of the fire is exceptionally soothing, carrying the healing effects into all life forms and removing toxins from the atmosphere. This entire ceremony, from set up time to completion, can be as brief as 20 minutes, or longer, depending upon the amount of supplies and other factors.

Why Do Agnihotra?

Do you experience that life has become more erratic and unstable?

Have you ever desired to help heal the planet?

Have you felt helpless as the environment appears to disintegrate around you, and wished you knew some positive action to take to help repair the damage done by humankind?

Have you wondered what you, as only one person, can do to make a difference?

Agnihotra is a solution. Anyone wishing to heal themselves, others, animals and plants, can do this fire ceremony. In doing so, you help rebalance the planet's resources, remove toxins from the environment and replenish the energy that supports all manifested existence, both animate and inanimate.

Who Can Perform This Ceremony?

Anyone with a sincere desire to live on this planet in a responsible manner can participate. People from many cultures, countries, spiritual traditions, and all ages are joining in this practice. Residents of Peru, Poland, the United States, Israel, Canada, Mexico, Hawaii, the Caribbean, Germany, Spain, West Indies, Australia and South Africa are only a sample of those I personally know who are dedicated to this simple daily practice. Male or female, young or elderly, educated or uneducated, wealthy or poor, well respected or unknown to the eyes of the world, you can practice this. It is not necessary to attend extensive training or to apprentice to a master fire keeper. You only need learn how to do it correctly and begin with heartfelt intention. It does require discipline, dedication and commitment. As with many worthwhile pursuits, as you do it the accumulated effects of the practice naturally encourage you to continue. Once you learn and practice it with regularity you can teach it to others. It is essential to maintain the purity of the ceremony and to not add new rituals that complicate it. Its beauty is in its simplicity. You do the simple act and let the divine universe create the results.

As with prayer, meditation, or other universal truth practices, no one owns this process. It belongs to nature and is to be freely shared. It is important to not charge a fee to those you teach. Of course you may accept donations that can be used to maintain your practice by paying for travel costs, venue rental, supplies, and equipment.

Do I Need Special Equipment?

Yes. And the equipment is easily obtained and affordable. In the next chapter I explain what you need and the procedural steps. The "Resources" chapter provides further references.

What Are the Benefits of Agnihotra?

Agnihotra fire ceremony affects the planet through the effects of the fire itself, its smoke, and the resulting ash. Purifying and soothing effects include but are not limited to:

People

Individuals living in an area where regular agnihotra fires are held report experiencing the following: increased peace of mind, enhanced sense of well-being and calm, release of addictions, improved relationships, renewed vitality, faster healing of wounds, dissolution of toxins, and a reduction in frequency of illness and physical distress. Testimonials report decreased or cessation of chronic illnesses such as asthma, diabetes, hypertension and others. Some scientific experiments indicate these reports are well founded. Persons who meditate regularly will experience deeper and more prolonged meditation, which in turn is increasingly proven to address hypertension, stress related illnesses and quality of living. Most amazing are studies indicating that agnihotra is uniquely capable of neutralizing the effects of radiation.

> One of my first agnihotra students lived with a cynical husband. He consistently made fun of her daily meditation, and now she was about to add "burning cow poo in a copper pyramid and chanting unintelligible words" to the mix! Undaunted, she began performing agnihotra on her back porch. Sure enough, she was teased. Her husband demanded she not tell friends or neighbors what she was doing, or they would "surely tote you away in a strait jacket, honey." One evening as she lit up her fire, he arrived to watch her perform, smoking his ever present cigarette. The next evening he returned and began joining her every evening. Nothing was said. She quietly observed and continued her practice. A month later he announced he was losing the desire to smoke and he eventually quit. Perform the fire and the fire creates the effects that are needed to bring balance.

Animals

Agnihotra effects on animals parallels the effects of human healing. Animals experience less illness, faster healing, calmer, more cooperative natures, and overall excellence of health. Disorders from years of neglect, herbicide and pesticide toxicity, antibiotics and other pharmaceuticals, and poor diet can all be reversed.

> One Sunday afternoon in late March, after four months of agnihotra practice at our home, our seventy-five pound German Sheppard, Pilot, got loose from his leash to race happily across a nearby busy boulevard. He was hit broadside by a car going forty-five miles per hour. He was tossed up over the hood of the car and through the air, landing with a 6 foot skid, hitting up against the street curb. The resounding "thud" brought neighbors running out to see what happened. My husband Ron ran over to pick up the injured dog. Yet before he could reach him, Pilot stood up, shook himself off, and trotted back toward our house, greeting Ron on the way with a wagging tail. He appeared fine! The next morning, other than some slight stiffness, he acted normal. We took him to our veterinarian to be thoroughly assessed. The vet said Pilot had light bruising but no broken bones, internal damage, or injuries. Amazed with our story, he inquired with dry humor, "Are you sure you aren't imagining this? I don't see any evidence that this dog was hit by a car!" Within a few days Pilot appeared normal; you'd never know he had been severely hit.

Plants

Plants grown in an agnihotra environment grow exceptionally large and abundant fruit. Some plants bear fruit multiple times during the season. Plants, and the resulting vegetables, fruit, nuts, or grains, are healthy and more nutritious. Such plants do not need chemicals, artificial fertilizers, herbicides or pesticides. Picked fruit and vegetables remain vital and healthy longer before spoiling. Soil that has been robbed of its vitality through use of artificial stimulants, over-production, or pollution, is replenished with agnihotra nutrients. Soil retains moisture better and plants utilize moisture more efficiently. Plants grown in an agnihotra atmosphere are less affected by drought. Science has demonstrated that agnihotra causes a change in the cellular structure of the plant, creating a more efficient distribution of nutrients, including moisture. Pests, fungus and molds, if present, remain in balance instead of overtaking the weakened plants as is typical with plants grown in an artificial, chemically-enhanced environment. "Homa Farming" utilizes agnihotra and other special fire ceremonies at specific times of the day, locating them at chosen places on the property. Agnihotra alone used morning and evening brings profound benefits. At sunrise and sunset time the pores of plants open, allowing the nourishing energy of the fire and smoke to enter more deeply. Resulting fire ash is utilized to heal plants and can replace fertilizer. Anyone pursuing organic or sustainable farming or gardening would do well to incorporate homa farming practices. Such scientifically proven methods enhance crop yield, healthy balance of beneficial insects, remove toxins from the soil, improve utilization of moisture, and enrich the beneficial microbial population. See the "Personal Agnihotra Stories" chapter to learn about the amazing benefits our plants and gardens have experienced. Refer to the "Resources" chapter to learn more about homa farming.

> A scrawny vine grew on a section of the chain link fence between our home and our neighbor's, barely hanging onto existence. Over the years neither she nor I ever saw it bloom. We did not know what kind of vine it was, but felt sorry for it so we both watered it to keep it alive. The spring following my first 4 months of daily agnihotra fires, the vine exploded exuberantly over the entire fence, with full lush leaves and beautiful small white blossoms. We never did figure out what the vine was, but all agreed it had experienced a miracle! Similar results enhanced our desert garden in Albuquerque, enlivening a diseased and dying apricot tree in the yard of our new home to rebound and subsequently yield richly flavored fruit in only one year.

Environment

Agnihotra purifies the atmosphere, soil, and water. As mentioned previously, it neutralizes radioactivity and toxins in the air. It expands the moisture-holding capability of air. As it heals the plants and re-establishes balance in nature, the environment heals. The ash resulting from the fire, when added to water, has been shown to purify it of harmful effects. Toxic rivers where ash has been distributed re-established a healthy eco-system.

Your home agnihotra helps remove toxins and heals the environment.

> Ron and I threw down our sleeping bags on an old bed in the vacant house, ready to settle in for the night. Our daughter was moving in the next day so we had vacuumed the living room, scrubbed bathrooms, and tomorrow would tackle the kitchen. One problem; the former resident had cats, lots of cats, who had generously left their signature odors throughout the house. Whew! We thought we could tolerate it for one night, but awoke a few hours later in full agreement that the odor was unbearable. Move to a nearby motel? Sleep in the car? Oh, wait! I had the perfect solution – do a fire ceremony! Wouldn't that be the true test of it shifting the environment? So I pulled out my fire kit. It wasn't sunrise or sunset, so I couldn't do agnihotra. But I knew another chant, the Gayatri mantra, which brings in cosmic light, so I set up my fire kit in the center hallway and began my ceremony. The sweet scent of its delicate smoke filled the house and we felt profound relief. Returning to bed, we slept soundly and arose the next day to a fragrant house. At sunrise I performed agnihotra. The ensuing cleansing smoke permeated walls and carpet, finalizing

the benefits. The cat odor was gone. Our daughter reported it never returned, and the house felt cleared of any lingering negative energy from previous inhabitants. Does your house stink after you burned the spinach on the stove? Did the water heater leak and the carpet padding smells musty as it dries? Did you have an experience in your home that you want dissolved from its energy field? Agnihotra provides sweet relief.

Soothing Remedy

Agnihotra atmosphere and ash are mentioned in ancient Vedic texts as a means of prevention and cure of diseases. Agnihotra and other fire practices are included with the many healing remedies presented in Ayurveda (Life-Knowledge). While not all claims have yet been tested by modern science, many have been substantiated. Agnihotra fire atmosphere and ash are purported to neutralize the effects on the body caused by ingesting radioactive foods or living in a radioactive environment. Agnihotra neutralizes pathogenic bacteria. It is an aid to drug and alcohol de-addiction. It harmonizes the functioning of Prana (life energy). Agnihotra is said to renew brain cells, revitalize skin and purify blood. Many people normally allergic to smoke experience a soothing effect when sitting in the smoke of agnihotra, including those suffering from asthma. Thousands of people in different parts of the world report personal relief from a great variety of ailments by sitting in the smoke of the ceremony. The effects of agnihotra are locked in the resulting ash which is then used as a natural healing remedy.

>At one of my first public agnihotra ceremonies, a woman with asthma approached me with concern, "What if the smoke antagonizes my asthma?" We decided she could sit by the door and if she noticed a problem, immediately leave. An asthmatic attack at my ceremony would not be an auspicious way to begin my agnihotra career! She sat through the ceremony but then immediately left, so I thought she was upset. The next day she came to my office to report the following: "I grew nervous when smoke filled the room, but found my lungs actually felt soothed! I expected spasms to start, but the soothing sensation continued. I was astounded and did not want to lose the effects. So I went right home and straight to bed with my inhaler handy on my nightstand as usual. I slept through the night! Do you know how long it has been since I did that? I cannot remember. I always wake up short of breath several times and need my inhaler. Okay, Ellie, now where can I get this fire kit?" After years of offering this ceremony, I now know that this is not an unusual occurrence; this is evidence to me that something beneficial is happening.

Psychotherapy

Agnihotra atmosphere removes stress and tension of the mind. It clears the mind of influential negative thought patterns. It allows one's innate intelligence to rise into awareness. It opens the mind to creativity and possibilities. Agnihotra leads to greater clarity of thought, improves overall health, increases energy, and allows the mind to fill with love. Its atmosphere promotes a deeper experience of meditation.

>Our warm-hearted neighbor faced each day with severe depression. He worked fewer and fewer hours at a job he had held for years, until one day he came home and stayed there, unable to interact with the world. His despondence deepened. One morning a policeman knocked on neighborhood doors instructing us to stay inside because our depressed neighbor was in his house with a gun, threatening to kill himself. He was calmed down and taken in for psychiatric assessment and subsequently assisted by doctors and counselors, to little avail. His distraught wife was exhausted from the daily turmoil of their lives and unsure what to do. About this time, I started daily sunrise and sunset practice of agnihotra. Within six weeks, his wife came to me one day with exciting news. "He starts back to work next week! All of a sudden, his motivation is returning. His psychiatrist and

his counselor are puzzled, because it seems his depression is unexpectedly dissolving. They don't know why, but who cares? I feel like we both just got our life back!" Was this due to agnihotra environment that now permeated our neighborhood? Or was some other unknown factor at work? I cannot prove it was the agnihotra, yet this was not an isolated incident, but only one of many that began to show up in our lives. There was only one consistent factor that I know was new in the mix of life: agnihotra.

In a world that is radically shifting into new ways of existence, where the future holds uncertainty for many, agnihotra offers unconditional vitality, health, protection, and support. So long as I have my fire kit, supplies and a dedicated heart, I can help.

What Happens Energetically?

Let's use the sunrise agnihotra as an example. At the precise time that the sun's rays first reach a specific location on our planet's globe, a shift in energy takes place. (The same happens in the evening as the last of the sun's rays depart.) During this brief time, the sun ray energy enhances the energetic effects of the ceremony. At the moment that chanting of the mantra begins and rice added, a powerful burst of energy surges out beyond Earth's atmosphere, and instantaneously returns, pulling rarified pure energy back down from space, sending it out in a *two mile radius. So long as that fire continues to burn, that energy field holds its integrity. This ancient science states that within that space, all negativity is neutralized. Toxins cease to be toxic, errant vibrations return to their original frequency, negative thinking, beliefs and habits are neutralized, distressed cells reestablish their original whole self-identity, and confusion is resolved. All that exists within that field of energy is affected in this manner, including the known and the unknown, the seen and the unseen, the physical, emotional, mental and spiritual.

> *When I first learned agnihotra, I heard the affected area had an eleven-mile radius. Then I heard it was a one-mile radius. When I asked a master teacher, he reported the effects had been scientifically measured at two miles. Because this energy is subtle, no doubt it influences far beyond this area, but at some point is too subtle to measure with our current scientific instruments.

Once the fire naturally burns out, the resulting energy is drawn down into, and stored in, the ash. For this reason, agnihotra ash is exceptionally beneficial. Morning agnihotra in a location affects the space positively and then gradually loses its effects during the day. Evening agnihotra re-establishes this energetic space which then gradually loses its effects overnight until the morning agnihotra. When agnihotra is repeated morning and evening of every day, the space becomes established in this energy. All that exists or visits this space is healed and divinely supported.

One who performs this agnihotra fire regularly in their home finds peace and serenity, cessation of physical distress or discord, and other abundant benefits. One who performs this not only benefits themselves and their household, but the entire community.

"...The yajnya confers fuller life and happiness. May this yajnya be performed everywhere. May the performer of the yajnya spread its knowledge. May the sacrificial fire keep us free from diseases..."

~ Yajur Veda: Chapter 1, Verse 22

> What if …
>
> Someone regularly performed agnihotra in every neighborhood?
>
> Every hospital had someone performing agnihotra daily and ash was used for healing?
>
> Agnihotra was taught and practiced at medical schools? … At all schools?
>
> Every prison performed agnihotra, and inmates were taught the practice?
>
> Every community had an agnihotra center where volunteers performed the ceremony daily, anyone could drop by for free to sit in on the ceremony, meditate, or rest for a while to release stress, heal, and find hope?
>
> Western scientists respected the experiments performed in other countries which provide evidence that agnihotra heals?
>
> *You* were the one in your community who performed it, taught it, and introduced it to any of the above organizations?

Origins of Agnihotra

This section promises to be a bit scholarly. However, it is helpful to recognize the early, authentic roots of the science of the Vedas (Sanskrit word for "knowledge").

Vedic science is ancient, revealed to enlightened beings possibly as early as 6,000 years ago. These ancient Vedas offer many sciences including but not limited to: fire (yajnya), light energy, sound, language (Sanskrit), astronomy, astrology (Jyotish), mathematics, healing the body-mind-spirit (Ayurveda), unifying the body-mind-spirit to achieve total enlightenment (Yoga), architecture, agriculture, animal husbandry, and design of one's living environment (Vastu). Such sciences do not stand alone but are intimately interwoven for ultimate balance. The science of agnihotra fire ceremony was lost during the ensuing centuries except to a select few who taught the tradition to chosen students, usually priests, who then carried the teachings into the present. It is reintroduced again now as a solution for a planet in peril. Originally agnihotra was a very complicated ritual relegated to males. One who performed agnihotra (the "hotri") carried the fire pyramid with him and was responsible for a myriad assortment of additional practices. It was simplified into this current, potent transformative practice by Shree Gajanan Maharaj, a revered saint who reintroduced it into the world as a science to be taught to all humankind. His disciples share it with others until it is now practiced across the planet.

Numerous ancient Vedic texts refer to yajnya (fire ceremony; also spelled yagnya), including but not limited to, Yajur Veda, Arthava Veda and Sama Veda. The Yajur Veda is a primary reference with several chapters devoted to this subject. Verses in this Veda indicate fire ceremony encourages rain, purifies food and water, increases health and vitality, encourages growth of food, and its resulting effects are spread far and wide into the universe.

Scientific Studies Are Available

Fire Ceremony has been practiced for thousands of years in multiple cultures. Many were highly complex societies as exemplified by ancient Sumeria, Egypt, Greece, India, China and Arabia. Such cultures offered sciences of astrology, medicine, and mathematics, to name a few. These sciences are authenticated today. While anyone who has experienced the benefits of these practices may not think such verification is needed, in the current world scientific proof is necessary to promote credibility. You can read of scientific studies online. Refer to "Resources" in this book. A most valuable and validating experiment is to practice agnihotra yourself for at least three months, observing the subtle changes in your own environment.

Fire Ceremony Word Definitions Explained

There are hundreds of fire ceremonies. Agnihotra is only one. It is fundamental, a beginning practice, and the foundation of all. Agnihotra has its roots in the Vedas which were originally taught orally and eventually written in the Sanskrit language. The simplest way to reference agnihotra is as "a purifying fire ceremony performed specifically at sunrise and sunset". For those with a more scholarly curiosity, I offer here some of the words associated with fire ceremony.

Yajnya (yah'-jn-yuh), *Yagnya, Yaga, Yaaga,* and *Yaag* are interchangeable forms of the same word that refers to any entire fire ceremony from start to finish (lighting the fire, chanting, giving offering into the fire, sitting until the fire burns out). Some of these events can be days or even weeks in length. When correctly spoken, it is "yajnya" but because the "j" and "n" together are difficult to pronounce, it becomes distorted. The original word in Sanskrit is pronounced yaah-jn (a very nasal "n")-yuh.

Havan (Hah'-vahn) and *homa* (Hoe'-muh) are interchangeable forms of the same word. They have the same Sanskrit root, *hu* which means "to offer". They represent giving an offering (oblation) into the fire (agni). Thus a havan or homa is the "offering" portion of the entire Yajnya process. The term *homa* is more commonly used in southern India and *havan* in the north. In common usage, these words are used in their various forms to refer to any fire ceremony. We might well say, "For havan's sake, let's get on with the ceremony!"

Agnihotra: Havan on Earth is my personal intention to help others spread the knowledge of this purifying practice across the planet Earth.

Chapter 3

How to Practice the Ceremony

Agnihotra is simple and, if you are organized, can be completed in 20-30 minutes. When you begin to add additional prayers or rituals, it can expand until it is not practical to do on a daily basis; or if these are added incorrectly, it dilutes or cancels this ceremony's effect. Please keep it simple as directed, so it can easily fit into your daily routine.

Required Basic Equipment and Supplies
(Resources are listed in another chapter)

• A copper pyramid	This must be of precise measurement
• A copper lid	To cover pyramid, if needed
• A copper stand	To protect surface from pyramid heat
• A copper spoon	Use to spread ghee on dung and for offerings
• Copper tongs	Used to add or adjust burning dung
• Dry cow dung	This is specially prepared to burn easily
• Ghee	Clarified butter, preferably organic
• Rice	Basmati rice, preferably brown, preferably organic
• Matches	Wooden kitchen matches are best
• Sunrise/Sunset chart (SR/SS)	One that is calculated for your zip code area and adjusted for daylight savings time
• Chant/prayer/mantra	Read off a printed paper until you memorize it
• Clock or Timer	One that counts the hour, minute and second; a small atomic-satellite clock is ideal

Equipment Examples

All pyramids will be shaped as shown. Other equipment and supplies may vary depending on the manufacturer.

Copper pyramid

Copper pyramid stand

Copper pyramid lid

Dried cow dung

Back row: matches, clock, time chart, ghee, rice
Front row: tongs, small spoon, large spoon, offering dish, dung

Agnihotra equipment at my outdoor fireplace. The fire burns in the pyramid inside the fire pit.

Abbreviated Instruction Version: Step by Step

1. Set up your space with the equipment and supplies
2. Practice silence
3. Spread ghee on the dung and place it in the pyramid
4. Prepare a narrow piece of dung as a "starter piece"
5. Start your fire three to five minute prior to the sunrise/sunset time
6. As the fire begins to build, mix ghee into your rice
7. Start the chant at the precise sunrise or sunset time (chants are listed in this chapter)
8. Offer the two pinches of rice; once at each "swaha"
9. Sit quietly meditating until the fire burns out.

Expanded Instruction Version: Step by Step (photos provided on the following pages)

1. First, it is essential to be willing to commit to the practice. The ideal is to do it twice daily. The reality is that you do it when you can, as often as you can. When you are committed to this as a priority, you begin to arrange events around it.

2. Set up your agnihotra ceremony space

    Choose a location in your home or yard where you can set up your pyramid, burn the fire, and be comfortably seated during the ceremony. For outdoor locations, seek a location out of the wind when possible, or create a protected fireplace (suggestions are included in this book).

3. Arrange with others in your household to not to disturb you and to practice silence during the time the fire is burning. The ceremony takes from 15-30 minutes, depending upon the length of time it takes for the fire to burn out.

4. Plan your schedule to be seated and ready to begin preparations 10 minutes before the sunrise or sunset time you will be performing.

5. Place your pyramid on its stand. Then place the following items nearby within arm's reach:

    a. Dried dung container

    b. Copper spoon and tongs

    c. Jar of ghee

    d. Jar of rice

    e. Box of wooden kitchen matches

    f. Old rag or towel nearby for wiping your hands

    g. Sunrise/sunset chart

    h. Clock that measures seconds

6. Place a pillow or stool in front of the fire pyramid to sit upon for comfort.

7. Sit quietly to center yourself so you can give full attention and intention to the process.

8. Empty the ash from your previous fire into a glass or ceramic storage jar or container.

9. Break the dung into small pieces so that you can fit at least 3-4 pieces in the pyramid for the fire. For a larger fire, use more dung.

10. Spread ghee onto each piece of dung. You may spread it on only one side, or both.

11. Place the dung into the pyramid in a manner so that air can flow around the pieces. An easy method is to place two pieces parallel on the square "floor" of the pyramid, and then place one or two more pieces crosswise on top of those. For a large fire, continue stacking pieces as high as you wish while assuring the stack remains securely balanced and allowing the air to circulate freely. Experiment until you find your best technique.

12. Choose a slender piece of dung for your "lighting stick". Spread ghee on it as well.

13. Before the sunrise/sunset time, light your lighting dung stick and place it into the center of the dung pieces, holding it until the pieces in the pyramid ignite and the fire begins to grow steadily. In humid climates or outdoors in cold weather, you may need to start your fire 8-10 minutes early. In dry climates or in warm weather, a 4-5 minute start time may be sufficient. Key point is to have a strong steady fire when you make your offering.

14. Between your thumb and forefinger of your right hand, pull out two pinches of rice.

15. Place the pinches of rice into a small copper offering bowl, or into your left hand.

16. Sort the rice with your right hand, tossing out any broken grains, leaving only whole grains for the offering.

17. Put a small amount of ghee onto the rice and mix it, making "snowballs". Or, if you prefer, melt a little ghee in the copper spoon over the fire, and pour it over the rice (be sure to let it cool a little first if mixing it in your hand). Another method is to melt ghee before the ceremony in a small copper vessel, using that to coat the dung pieces and rice.

18. At precisely sunrise/sunset time, begin the appropriate chant. *Chant it only* **one** *time*.

19. When you chant the first "swaha" toss or drop one pinch of prepared rice, coated with ghee, directly into the fire. Use your right hand to make this fire offering, even if you are left-handed. (Sacred offerings are made with the right hand, representing positive energy.)

20. At the second "swaha" toss the second pinch of rice onto the fire.

21. Sit quietly, meditating on the fire or with closed eyes, until the fire burns out.

Agnihotra Chants

Morning Sunrise Agnihotra chant

Sooryáya swáhá

sooryáya idam na mama

prajápataye swáhá

prajápataye idam na mama

Evening Sunset Agnihotra chant

Agnaye swáhá

agnaye idam na mama

prajápataye swáhá

prajápataye idam na mama

Setting up for agnihotra

Spreading ghee on dung piece. Break pieces as needed to fit into the pyramid.

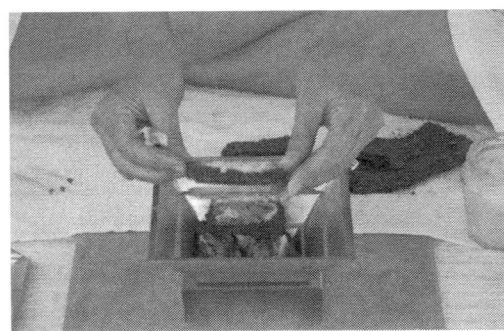

Placing "buttered" dung pieces into pyramid. Notice they are placed to allow air flow.

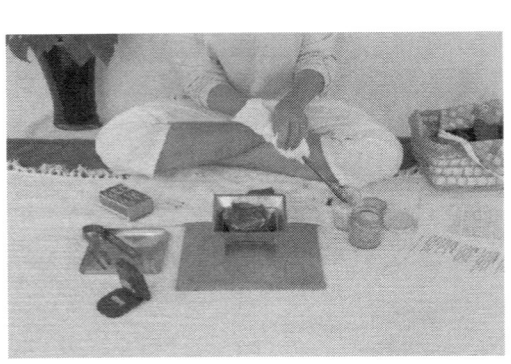

I keep an old hand towel handy to wipe ghee and ash residue off my hands.

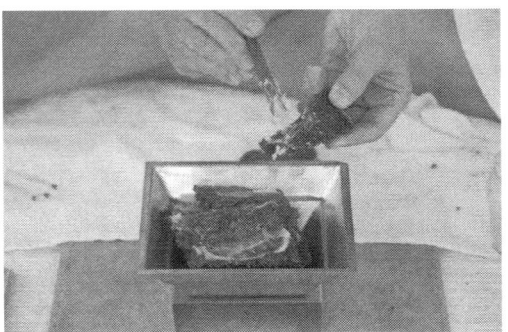

For your "lighting piece" choose a slender piece of dung to "butter" with the ghee.

AGNIHOTRA: HAVAN ON EARTH

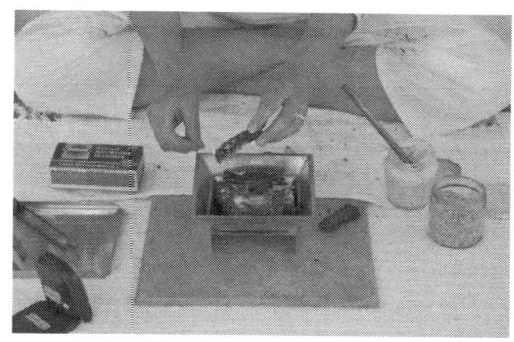

Lighting the "lighting piece"

Inserting the "lighting piece" into the prepared dung in the pyramid

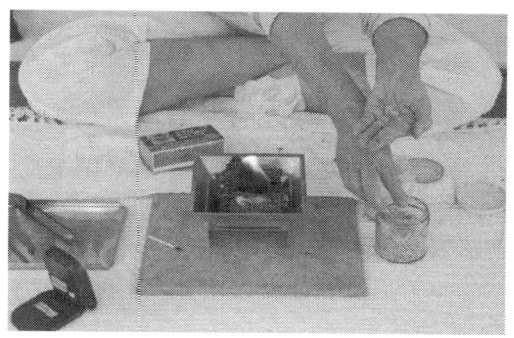

Gathering two pinches of rice. Cull out the broken pieces and discard.

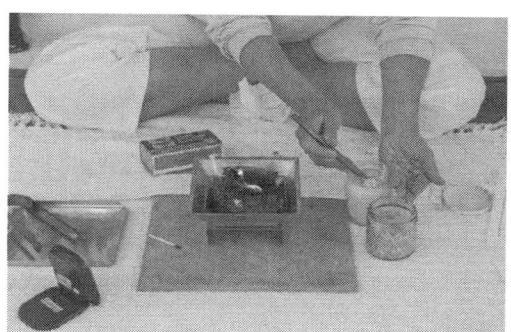

Add ghee to coat the rice.

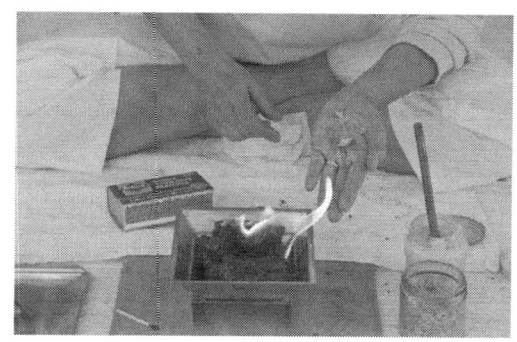

Divide the rice into two portions.

At precise time, begin the chant. Drop one portion of coated rice into fire with each chanted "swaha".

Sit silently to meditate until the fire burns out. This concludes your Agnihotra.

Learning the Chant

In the "Resources" section of this book helpful websites are listed where you can listen to the mantras to learn correct pronunciation and the tune. You may also contact me at CosmicGathering@gmail.com or via my website www.CosmicGathering.com. Leave me your name and a phone number with voicemail where I can call and sing the morning and evening chants. Listen to them until memorized, and on a mobile phone you can carry it to your fire site for practice. An audio-visual version will be added to my website in the future.

The correct pronunciation is very important; thus it is essential to be taught personally or listen to an audio recording. Don't let the unfamiliar language scare you; it is actually quite simple to learn and rolls off the tongue easily. Notice that the morning and evening mantras use the exact same words except for the first and third words of each. The morning "Sooryaya" refers to the transformational energy of fire. The evening "Agnaye" refers to the transformational energy of the sun. The fire and sun in this context represent the divine transformational fire (energy), not the specific physical fire or sun. The sun as we know it serves, among other reasons, as a transformer which changes cosmic energy into a form that is best utilized by the physical aspects of our planet.

A General Translation of the Chants

If you are like me, you don't want to speak words unless you know what they mean. I list here general translations. As with all language translations, each Sanskrit scholar or teacher is confident that his or her translation is the correct one. I have heard four slightly varied translations, each from someone I respect. It helps to be reminded that the "heart" of the words is what is important. If we are thinking of the chant's literal meaning when chanting it, we are "in the mind" which limits the experience. If we instead focus on the rhythm and beauty of the word's sounds, we transcend the mind and are carried to a higher vibrational experience. Basically the chant offers recognition of the divine transformational energy represented by the sun or fire. It is a confirming statement that "I am not *this* existence; but am an expression of *That*."

Morning Chant Meaning

To this fire I offer everything. This offering belongs to the Divine, not to me.

Evening Chant Meaning

To the sun I offer everything. This offering belongs to the Divine, not to me.

Examples of Where You Can Practice

Patio or Porch

I practice outdoors on my patio. For years I have set my pyramid in a clay chiminea (Mexican portable clay stove with chimney) which helps protect it during wind or wet weather. When not in use, a small clay flower pot saucer fits nicely as a cover for the top of the chimney to keep out rain and snow. The pyramid stand, pyramid and lid are used and stored in this little stove. I sit comfortably on a folded blanket in front of my chiminea to perform the ceremony. I use two large "storage" pots nearby which I created from red clay planting pots; the lids are large clay saucers sized large enough to fit snugly onto the top. To the immediate right is a pot which stores a handy supply of dried dung. To my left is a pot which holds the rice

A clay chiminea fireplace

and ghee jars, spoon and tongs, matches, clock sunrise/sunset chart and an old towel. I am a neatnik, so I use this towel to place under my supplies as I prepare the fire. It catches any spilled rice, ghee, and dung crumbs and then I shake it out over my nearby garden before putting things away. I purchased several large ceramic countertop flour/sugar canisters at a second hand store which I use to store the ash until it is eventually sifted and used. Glass jars will suffice as well. These are placed next to the chiminea for convenience. When desired I can remove the pyramid from the chiminea to place on a ceramic tile for a ceremony. I do this for group events, so multiple people can observe or participate with fire.

A few years ago I created a weatherproof brick fireplace from extra supplies we had laying around our yard. All you need is non-metal building materials that are fire and weather proof. See the chapter "Build a Simple Outdoor Fireplace" for instructions. Originally this was placed on my patio. Eventually, I created a special havan nook for it in the back corner of our yard.

An easy to assemble brick and tile fireplace

A special havan nook in the corner of our yard

Apartment, Condo

In our first apartment, I placed my fire pyramid on a 12x12 ceramic tile on our second floor balcony. To keep the wind from blowing out my fire, I created a three-sided cardboard wind/visual barrier, cut from a large box. This was clamped to the sides of my wooden balcony. Then we moved to a two-story condo and I purchased the clay chiminea to set out on our balcony.

Living Room Fireplace

When first learning agnihotra, we lived in a house with a large fireplace. I placed two attractive baskets by the fire place; one for dung, the other for supplies. I performed the agnihotra in the fireplace, opening the damper first to pull the resulting smoke up and out of the house. This minimized any soot residue from building up in the house. The house smelled heavenly and the smoke drifted out to heal the yard and neighborhood.

See "Location" in the following chapter, and FAQs, for additional suggestions.

Notes

Chapter 4

Explanation of Ceremony Components

This book presents information from my personal experience and research. I limit my teaching to the simplest scientific essentials of agnihotra.

There are countless variations and ways to perform agnihotra that include additional ritual and requirements. I fully respect teachings of each of these traditions. I have personally received information and training from multiple teachers. My observation is that agnihotra practice can easily be complicated by personal preferences. If three honorable teachers instruct with different processes, yet each asserts his or her way is the only proper one, then are there thousands of people who are doing it wrong? I think not, because the results of these people's experience is proof the teachers' methods of doing the fire is working. Therefore, I endeavor to present the process stripped of any non-essential steps. If you have been taught by a lineage or another teacher, please honor their instructions and bask in the benefits you experience. As one who has offered spiritual teachings to people for over 20 years, I chuckle to think of the many people I've taught who complain about religious differences destroying the true intent of spiritual practice, yet they immediately attach to "their way" of agnihotra, meditation, form of exercise, or any newly enthused practice they learn. They promptly proceed to then judge other methods, the very reason they discarded religion! It seems our journey of being open to clear truth is filled with many obstacles.

Location

- Preferably, you use the same location for each ceremony. Repetition in the same area creates a sustained purifying energy field. If you need to change locations you may do so.

- It does not matter which direction you face to bring results.

  Some people like to face east; others like to face the direction of the sun. There are subtle influences facing any direction. Knowing this, you may have preferences. I sit facing whichever direction is best for my pyramid arrangement or the event. When I performed agnihotra in a home with a fireplace, I faced south. In a home with an outdoor courtyard, I faced east. On an apartment balcony I faced north. In classrooms or event halls, I face the audience. When performing it in a sick room, I face the recipient's chair or bed.

- If done indoors, the smoke causes soot to build up on walls and furniture. If you have a fireplace, open the damper and perform it in the pit so that most smoke rises up the chimney. Sufficient smoke remains in the home to benefit. One of my fire teachers sets aside a room in his home where he and his family perform the ceremony. Each family member has an individual pyramid. This is a beautifully inspiring model to me. Soot accumulates in that one room which can be cleaned if necessary. Some people I know empty a closet, perform it there and then clean and repaint it if they move. If your home lacks a fireplace, perform it outside on a covered porch or patio, or any suitable flat surface. In apartments, perform it outside on a patio or balcony. See the "How to Practice" chapter for additional suggestions.

Chanting Prayers

- Everything consists of vibrating energy and thus everything is affected by vibration. Any sound vibration affects the surrounding area. A chanted prayer creates a precise vibration which creates a precise energetic shift. We intuitively hum a soft tune to soothe a child. Clapping hands enliven us. Shrill yelling disrupts the nervous system. Lilting song lifts our spirits. Specific chants likewise create expected outcomes.

- This specific chanted prayer (mantra) sets up a vibration that heals. When combined with other ingredients of the ceremony, this vibration transmutes the vibration of the entire area into a purified zone which remains, slowly diffusing, until the following sunrise or sunset. With regular repetition, the area is permeated with this healing resonance.

- I prefer to know the meaning of words I voice. I do not want to speak words contrary to my beliefs. However, it is not necessary to know what a chant means in order to experience results. In fact, if you focus on the meaning of the words you bring your mind into the process instead of simply tuning into the vibration which is more subtle than thought. During the initial four months when I was learning I did not know the meaning of the words, yet results were forthcoming. Only later did I learn the meaning and realized it was not essential. For those who wish to know, translation of the words is provided elsewhere in this book.

- Try a simple experiment with sound vibration.

   Our daughter did the following experiment for her middle school science fair project. If you have doubts of the effects of vibration, try this yourself! She purchased three small cabbage plants of equal size. (Three similar plants of the same species is required.) Each was placed in a window with similar light. The first was placed next to a radio playing classical music 24 hours a day. The second was placed next to a radio playing hard rock 24 hours a day. The third was placed in a window with no music and only the sounds of birdsong, insects and wind were heard. Within three days the one near classical music bent toward the radio, the one near hard rock music bent away, and the one with no music remained upright. Within two weeks, the one near classical music draped gracefully over the radio as if to embrace the music, leaves were large and it was the healthiest of the three plants. The one near hard rock music dramatically bent away from the radio; it was quite small and spindly. The one with no music continued to grow upright and was mid-sized. At the end of three weeks the one near the hard rock music was nearly dead, the one near classical music thrived, and the third one was also healthy. We then stopped the experiment because we no longer wanted to torture the hard rock music plant!

Practice Silence

- Provide silence so that the chant vibration and the resulting energy are not distorted by loud noises or talking.
- If your only option is to do the ceremony where traffic, talking neighbors or dog barking is unavoidable, you may still do so. For two years we lived where our yard backed up to a busy city thoroughfare with cars, delivery trucks, police sirens and motorcycles racing by at all hours. Definitely not a quiet environment! Yet agnihotra brought beautiful results to our yard and neighborhood. I enjoyed envisioning the soothing energy sweeping over each vehicle zooming through our healing zone, bringing the occupants a momentary divine pause in their unsuspecting lives.

Dung

- If you can, use dung dried and prepared specifically for fire ceremony. This dung is collected while fresh and shaped and dried into convenient pieces that are easy to work with and burn well. Fresh dung prepared in this manner is free of insect critters, so is more pure and the fire does not burn up some bug's cozy little home. Directions for preparing dung are included in another chapter of this book. If you cannot find prepared dung or do not have money to purchase it, you may collect dried field dung from a local farmer. Assure the cows are fed a quality diet, are well treated, and the dung is free of sand and dirt.
- Store your dung supply in a cardboard box, paper sack, straw basket or natural cloth bag in your garage or a rainproof shed. Store it in the home if you need to; just realize the aroma of the dry dung will cling to the area. People often find the scent pleasant. Do not store it in plastic, or metal containers unless they are made of gold or copper, which is unlikely for most of us!
- Dung varies in quality. Texture and density depends on the condition of the original dung when it was set out to dry or what the cow had been eating. It may be hard as a rock or it may include more ingested grasses and be softer. If it is hard you may need to add more ghee. I once had really hard dung that just wouldn't light; I spread ghee on both sides of the entire batch and stored it that way, allowing it to soak. Upon use I again spread fresh ghee. This helped it burn. A woman I know took her hard dung out to the garage, put it in a vice, and sawed it into smaller pieces! Whatever works!
- Dried dung may be anywhere from 1/4 inch to 1/2 inch thick. I've been able to work with any thickness they offered. I'm just thankful they do the collecting for me!

Ghee

Ghee is clarified butter. You can easily make your own or purchase it. If possible use organic ghee. A simple recipe for making ghee is included in this book.

Rice

Preferably use brown basmati rice available at most health food stores. If it is not available use any brown rice. If brown is not available use white rice. Use the whole grain, sorting out and discarding broken grains. The whole grain provides the entire energy field of the rice while a broken grain is a distorted energy field.

Sunrise-Sunset Time

- It is essential to use a chart that lists the specific sunrise and sunset times for your zip code area. Several organizations provide these, and are listed in the "Resources" chapter. They offer free download programs for calculating your own, with full instructions. You may also order the prepared chart. If you have a smart phone, download an Agnihotra App that adjusts to time changes, to your current location if you travel, and has an alert alarm feature.

- *The sunrise and sunset times listed in your local paper, television or radio are not correct for this purpose.* Sunrise and sunset time is calculated by different methods. Because the earth's atmosphere distorts what you see along the horizon, when you see the rising sun, it has not actually risen yet. The opposite is true at sunset. You want time that is precisely correct for the location of your ceremony, one that is calculated and timed with a satellite clock. You want the time calculated down to the second. Ideally, you use a small atomic/satellite clock that counts seconds. Your cell phone is correct to the minute, but not the second. In a pinch you can use it and when the correct minute registers you then start counting seconds until the precise second is reached.

- There is only a brief time span when the energy of the sun provides an energetic "boost" that causes the agnihotra effect. So it is essential to be prepared ahead of time and concise with the timing.

- The question arises, "If this is an ancient science, how did they calculate the correct time thousands of years ago before satellite clocks were invented?" Good question! I wondered the same thing. It turns out, not surprisingly, that in those days life was quieter and one who practiced the ceremony was tuned to the rhythms of nature. This practitioner comprehended the shift in subtle energy indicating the precise timing. As a young girl growing up on a farm, I often recognized a "magical moment" in the morning when the quality of bird song altered and I noticed a "quickening" of the sounds and smells outside my window. One of my fire teachers said this was the precise moment of sunrise. Upon occasion I prepare for agnihotra sufficiently early to enjoy a few moments of waiting time. At a precise instant I noticed a subtle shift in the energy, an enhancement of the vitality of plant life and bird song. If observing plants closely, I see their leaves slightly quiver. Agnihotra teachers also say at the time of sunrise or sunset, in a healthy person the breath is moving equally through both nostrils. (I consider myself healthy, but this technique has not proven true in my personal experience.)

Chapter 5

Frequently Asked Questions

I know that the minute this book goes to print, another question will show up! If I don't address your concern here, please email me; I can add your question and the response to book updates. There are so many questions to ask and such a variety of responses from the myriad of havan teaching traditions available, that it is impossible for me to represent all the possible views. Therefore, I respond here from personal experiences of myself and fellow fire practitioners. As I mention frequently in this book, if you are taught differently from a teacher or tradition you honor, you may confidently to follow their guidelines.

Why do you call these fire ceremonies *havan*? I thought they are commonly referred to as *homa* or *yagnya*?

Because I love the Sanskrit word *havan*! Its meaning is the same as *homa* or *yagnya*, yet resounds as does heaven or haven, two related words we are all familiar with that denote peace, compassion, sanctuary, and divine connection. It is a comfortable word to westerners who do not know or care to know Sanskrit. When I heard this word as an option, I felt absolute delight. See "Fire Ceremony Word Definitions Explained" in chapter 2 for further explanation.

What can go wrong with the ceremony?

Everything. Especially in the beginning of your practice when you are still learning the art. I'll use my personal experience to elaborate! You might start the fire only to watch it burn out before it is time to chant. You can absent mindedly sing the morning chant in the evening or vice versa. You can strike match after match and none of them stay lit. Your dung lighting-piece can refuse to burn. Your dung can be difficult to burn. You might start a beautiful fire only to have a gust of wind blow it out. You can start the fire and forget to prepare the rice. What do you do when these happens? You patiently smile, acknowledge that no one is perfect, and toss the remains of that fire onto the garden. My mother said the Divine has a wonderful sense of humor. This is a good time to believe her. Remember that you offered it with loving intention; next time you can get it right.

What should be my attitude when performing agnihotra?

Be joyful and happy! Be attentive, purposeful, and focused. Practice with gratitude and appreciation for good things in your life and expect more to unfold. Welcome it into life as another spiritual or healing practice, along with prayer, meditation, yoga, tai chi, reading from authentic writings, service to others, or whatever you find supportive. Don't be frowning, demanding perfection, self-judging, critical of how others perform it, prideful of your practice, or afraid to fail. Relax and surrender to the process. As with all new practices, whether learning to drive a car, play tennis, or blow your first bubble with bubblegum, with consistent practice you become proficient and it becomes second nature.

A regular practice of agnihotra with commitment and patience is a good foundational practice for spiritual living! Who among us has always done it right? Certainly I have not; there are times I've felt the only thing I have perfected is imperfection! Haven't we done the best we can in the moment, based on who we are at that time and our current level of understanding? Haven't we missed the mark sometimes, causing ourselves even more hassles to resolve? Didn't we learn from this - what worked and what did not - and resolve to do it more wisely next time? This is how our experiences in life expand understanding, leading to deeper insights. In every moment, choose "who" you will be and then what you will do. Then act. Observe the results; what worked and what did not? Learn so you can adjust for the next time. Improve and continue your cycle of expansion. Act, observe, learn, adjust, and act again with adjustments. In the future you can stand back and admire the results!

Practice agnihotra and observe the results for yourself.

Are there any circumstances when I should not perform agnihotra?

If you are severely ill with a contagious disease…

In such circumstances it is recommended to not perform it for others, but the fire is beneficial for you, so you may do it for yourself. A cancer patient I know was advised to do it daily without fail. Her testimony indicates it helped, however there is no research to verify her claim. Because the ash is used for healing, it is suggested that your breath and any disease it carries should not be transferred to the fire. My observation (not scientifically proven) is that such breath would be purified by the fire. Self-reference this and make your own decision.

Women, when experiencing menses…

This is highly debated and no matter what I say here, I will upset someone! It helps to realize there are two sides to every "story". Any teaching has an element of possible truth within it, yet can also have been influenced away from original intent. Remember that this ceremony causes subtle effects which are not physical in nature. One of my master teachers was strongly opposed to performing it during menses and I respect his strict adherence to what his lineage taught. I know of no scientific reasoning behind this, yet there are a few explanations that are plausible. One is that during fire ceremony, energy flows upward toward the cosmos. During menses, energy flows downward toward earth. These two competing energies create an energy block which could cause the energetic effects of the fire ceremony to lessen. Another explanation is that the upward energy flow during fire ceremony can stall or stop the woman's natural downward flow and thus stop or diminish the menses blood flow. Some hatha yoga practitioners, who practice breathing techniques to alter energy flow, find that techniques moving energy upward may block or stop menses flow. A few traditions still teach that women are "impure" during menses but there is no scientific or legitimate anecdotal evidence to support such a claim. The issue of whether women have been discounted, and not allowed to perform sacred ceremony in many traditions, is a topic of discussion for another book. How have I chosen to address this? Before I was told this feature of agnihotra, I performed during menses with tremendous results. Once I was informed, I continued to do so but used that ash only for my garden. Agnihotra is a loving, empowering ceremony for anyone, and not to be distorted by anger or judgment. Use your own Divine-given discernment to make your decision.

Can women actually practice Vedic fire ceremony?

> Concerning women performing havan, during one of my agnihotra teaching seminars, one of the participants was an East Indian medical doctor, also trained in Ayurvedic healing and Vedic philosophy. He shared with us that in ancient times women performed havans. Then power shifted to male dominance and this was removed from the feminine arena. In the eighth century a highly respected Indian spiritual philosopher taught that such separation of women from participation with divine ritual was a great delusion being manifested upon human consciousness. Some women again began practicing havan but it was still not accepted in greater society. Now it is again accepted by many. I personally embrace my opportunity to perform all spiritually expansive practices when my heart guides me to do so. In essence, we are neither male nor female, but a blending of two marvelous energies that create the balanced whole.

I am an ex-convict…outcast…failure in life…sinner…misunderstood person. Can I practice this?

> Absolutely! Please do. Each of us has taken actions we later regret. Be assured that this will help heal you and offer a way for you to mend any damage your experiences have created. As you heal, any repercussions from your life choices will heal as well, through the ripple effect.

What is a *kunda*?

> *Kunda* is the Sanskrit word for the pyramid in which a ceremonial fire is burned. Most frequently, a metal pyramid is used. Agnihotra uses one of specific geometric measurements, made only of copper or gold. Although kundas are usually square in shape, they may be in other shapes or made of other materials, depending upon the desired effects of the ceremony.

Is a *puja* the same as a havan?

> Puja usually refers to a sacred ritual for the purpose of connecting with the Divine. It may include a havan, but is more. Puja frequently includes numerous practices which may include special prayers, havan, chanting, bowing, gestures, use of various foods or herbs, and devotions to a deity. Events in other traditions which are similar are the Jewish Passover meal, Native American sun dance, and Christian taking of communion.

Does ash from the previous fire need to be removed from the pyramid before starting a new fire, or is it okay to keep building new fires on top of ash?

> I recommend you remove ash from the previous fire. I empty it into my glass ash storage jar before I place dung in for the new fire. This way, if my new fire has any problems, and is not successful, its ash is not mixed in with a previously successful fire's ash.

If some of my dung or rice doesn't burn through, can I re-use it in the next fire?

> It is recommended to not re-use it. I toss it onto my garden.

If the fire has gone out but there is a lot of smoke, can I put the lid on the pyramid and consider the "session closed"?

You can if it is necessary to move on with your day (which I often need to do!). However if you have time it is beneficial to sit and breath in the smoke which carries benefits deep into your body cells through breath. It also can permeate the neighborhood. Remember, this smoke heals.

I am left-handed. Why do I have to use my right hand?

According to many traditions, energy emitted from the right and left hand differs. Energy of the right hand is favored for making an offering. This is why we place our right hand over the heart when making a pledge, or extend our right hand to another in friendship. And in some cultures, the right hand is considered the "public" hand. I do sympathize with all you left-handers who need to constantly adjust! To my knowledge, effects of right-handed vs. left-handed offerings have never been scientifically assessed for fire ceremony. And if you were missing your right hand, I would heartily suggest you use your left hand and trust the healing effects of the ceremony to take care of the situation!

I am afraid of the fire burning me when I offer the rice.

While offering it with your right hand is recommended, you may also use your copper spoon in your right hand. This allows you to place the rice into the flame without fear of being burned. There are many additional havans in which offerings of melted ghee are given with the copper spoon.

Can I use a butane lighter instead of a wooden match to light my starter piece?

I was taught to use a wooden match, as butane gas in a lighter adds an unwanted ingredient to the fire. However someone recently asked me if sulphur from a wooden match didn't also add an unwanted ingredient? Help! Okay…I'll just use a wooden match as I was taught and let it go at that. I don't have time to go out and find two flint rocks to strike together!

Can I use camphor pellets to help ignite the fire?

I was taught to not use camphor, as it adds an unwanted ingredient to the fire. However, many fire practitioners are taught to use camphor for fire ceremony. A primary reason is to help ignite a strong fire. I never found it necessary. You can easily light fire with only dung and ghee. If your fire doesn't start easily, consider dropping a small glob of ghee down into the center to help it ignite more quickly. An additional caution about camphor; it is harmful if inhaled excessively. Once when cleaning the fire kit of a practitioner who used small camphor pellets for his fires, I emptied pellets from their jar into a bowl so I could wash out the jar. I breathed the scent of the pellets for ten minutes in his small kitchen as I completed the task. Within three hours I was severely chilled and by the next morning required emergency treatment from my Oriental medicine doctor to re-establish my internal body heat. My lungs were damaged and breathing was shallow for several months. Camphor is also used medicinally for a variety of purposes; just know what you are doing when using it.

Can I add herbs, sweet grass, sage or other special ingredients?

Not for agnihotra. Keep it simple as instructed. Please. There are always variations in teachings, so there may be special circumstances I am not aware of that do use herbs during agnihotra. Certainly there are other fire ceremonies where such additional ingredients are added. While I have performed some, I do not consider myself sufficiently knowledgeable to teach more than a few.

Can I "charge" my crystals and stones with this energy? How about my essential oils and other healing remedies?

> Yes. You can place crystals, oils or other special items near the pyramid. Over time they become "charged" with the beneficial energy. Agnihotra fire energy can transform undesirable energy in objects into healing energy. The Vedic tradition includes healing with crystals, precious metals and essential oils.

Crystals, jewelry, and healing remedies can be infused with agnihotra's beneficial vibration.

If I sing the chant multiple times, won't it be more powerful?

> No, absolutely not. You would then be chanting after the influence of sunrise/sunset time has ceased. Keep it simple as instructed and do not overcomplicate this or start adding to it - please! Overcomplicating becomes burdensome after initial enthusiasm wears off and discouragement sets in. In some other fire ceremonies, continuous chanting is desirable. However, with agnihotra you only chant it once and then sit in the silence, allowing benefits to unfold.

What if I don't pronounce the Sanskrit words properly?

> Listen to a recording carefully. Seek to hear the precise sounds and emphasis. Then sing according to what you hear, let go, and trust. At that point, the intention carries your ceremony to fruition. Even priests who were taught complicated ceremonies since childhood, who are steeped in the tradition and chant havans in sacred temple events, can disagree on how to pronounce the words. A woman who attended a holy ceremony in India tells me she watched as five priests argued for two hours on how to pronounce two words in a common Sanskrit chant that is sung in ashrams and yoga studios all over the planet! If those who are considered authorities cannot agree, why do we worry? Choose a version and chant with brilliance of confidence. Observe the beneficial effects! There is not some Divine being who hovers overhead to listen, judge and then say, "No, you didn't stress that syllable correctly, so your havan won't work. Get it right next time!"

Can I sing the agnihotra words in English (French, German, Italian, Spanish, Hebrew…)?

> No. Agnihotra is to be chanted in Sanskrit. It is the vibration of these specific sounds that combines with the other ceremony elements to create healing results.

Can I sing a prayer in my own language while burning a fire?

> Yes! It would not be agnihotra but certainly would be beneficial. Prayers are sung with fire ceremonies in many cultures. I encourage you to create your own ceremony! Prayer has definite beneficial effects. To add a fire ceremony to it supports those effects. The "Prayer of Saint Francis" has long been a guiding light to me and I have chanted it repetitively along with a fire, experiencing a joyful connection expanding within me. A prayer in any language holds the vibration of your loving devotion. This then becomes a sacred practice.

Can I sing other chants before or after agnihotra?

> Yes. However, this would be an exception, offered when doing a longer ceremony at sunrise or sunset time. I personally prefer to let agnihotra stand on its own. The energy of this is so powerful; I believe it accomplishes any additional purpose that you might want to experience from a particular event.

However, I do occasionally include it with other events if sunrise or sunset time falls within the event's time frame. Again, may I emphasize to keep this simple and to practice agnihotra until you become established with it as part of your life, and only then to begin adding other ceremony.

If I perform agnihotra inside a building, how does it get outside to my yard and neighborhood?

Agnihotra creates a subtle energetic effect that is not physical; it is not contained by walls or even mountains.

How can I perform it outdoors during inclement weather?

On sunny and calm days there is no problem doing it outdoors. During windy weather, create a wind break out of plywood sheets or cardboard; or perform it in a chiminea or outdoor fireplace (see "How to Practice" chapter for details). Set up your kit under a roofed area if available. If you have a garage, perform it inside near a slightly opened door. Smoke drifts outside leaving you free from rain and wind. I have also performed it inside our home near an open door in the same manner. Remember that wherever you do it within a roofed or walled area, soot eventually builds up on the structure.

If I can't do agnihotra at sunrise/sunset time, can I do it at another time? It's always sunrise/sunset somewhere on the planet, isn't it?

It must be done at sunrise or sunset when they occur at the location where you perform the ceremony. If done at another time, it is a nice ceremony that bestows some benefits, but it is not agnihotra ceremony and does not offer its balancing and healing effects. Precisely at sunrise and sunset there are specific energies present in the atmosphere that are working with the ceremony to enhance its results.

What if I can't do it regularly?

Do it when you can. Agnihotra is a priority for me in the morning and weekends. During short winter days I cannot do it if I am at work locations at sunrise or sunset times. When traveling I may be enroute at those times. During late spring, summer, and early fall it is easier to arrange my mornings and evenings. The more frequently you practice, the more accumulated benefits are experienced.

How much dung should I order/make?

I usually order three pounds which is roughly one brown paper grocery bag full. You can order that much from suppliers if they have it available. When I will be really active doing multiple ceremonies, I order six pounds, but that is much more than most people doing it at home would find necessary.

What do I say when people ask what fuel I am using?

You might use the Sanskrit word for cow dung chips, which is "gomay". But then they will ask what gomay is, I suppose. I just spit it out … "cow dung", and then add that it is used for fuel in many cultures. Homesteaders who crossed the prairie in covered wagons used buffalo dung for fuel, as there were no trees for wood. In the famous book series, "Little House on the Prairie", the Ingalls family burned buffalo dung. If that cute little Laura Ingalls grew up using dung for fuel, I don't see why we can't do so!

Wild bee on Mullein blossoms

Let me make a complete fool of myself here…I first heard the term "gomay" used at a sacred fire ceremony and when I went home, incorrectly remembered it as "mopay". So, I stored my agnihotra dung in cardboard boxes in our garage, which I diligently labeled "mopay". I still use my "mopay" boxes. It keeps me from being overly enthralled with myself! Within yourself, confirm that agnihotra transforms earthy cow dung into a subtle energy that vitalizes herbs, nourishes wildlife, and blesses the planet.

If I want to burn bigger fires to create more ash, should I purchase a bigger pyramid?

No. You simply stack dung higher in your small pyramid. You can go online to see beautiful photos of amazingly tall fires. The dung holds its shape as it burns and retains this stacked form until you stir it into ash dust.

Will the fire's smoke hurt my lungs or burn my eyes?

Agnihotra fire smoke is gentle and mild. It smells sweetly fragrant and is easily inhaled. People with lung issues such as asthma frequently report their breathing is improved in this smoke's environment. This smoke is highly refined and testimony indicates the body interprets it as soothing, unlike smoke of a wood fire which is acrid and burning to lining of the nose, throat and lungs. Those who perform any extensive Vedic fire ceremonies are encouraged to do so in well-ventilated areas, or outdoors.

I know someone who says smoke from dung fires causes cancer.

I have practiced this ceremony for years and talked with dozens of others who have also practiced it. Not one of them has reported experiencing cancer. Additionally, I have heard countless stories of people being cured of cancer with use of purifying fires, a few of which are scientifically authenticated. It is possible that someone who is not fully informed, but well intentioned, would find cancer-causing agents in burned dung; however fire ceremony combines the energetics of multiple ingredients such as sound intonation and timing along with the dung, combining them into a new alchemically changed form which is unlike simple burned dung. If one regularly sits in on extended fires within an enclosed environment, in time it could distress the lungs. This will not happen with simple agnihotra.

Do I need to make my own ghee?

No. You may purchase quality ghee at most natural food stores. Some people find that making ghee is a beautiful part of doing fire ceremony, and a recipe is included in this book. You may go online to search for additional recipes. With my full schedule, making my own ghee at home is not a priority choice. Because of the number of fire ceremonies I perform, I would be making ghee every weekend!

Why is brown rice preferred?

Brown rice contains the bran, and is unpolished, thus it includes the entire, potent energy field of the rice grain. Some respected traditions alternately prefer white rice because of its pure color.

How do I clean my copper pyramid?

Ash and ghee do eventually build up a coating. I gently scrape the extra build-up off with a knife, being careful to not scrape down to the bare metal. You don't want to scrape off the copper, and repeated metal scraping would change the pyramid's shaping. Any scrapings can be added to your plants. Do not wash it with soap or harsh cleansers. As you perform the ceremony, the pyramid begins to build an energetic field which you do not want to remove by washing. From repeated use, even the outside a the new, shiny copper pyramid loses its luster and turns dark. This is to be expected.

Is it necessary to bathe before doing agnihotra?

A "purist" teaches that everyone should shower/bathe before any fire ceremony, or any spiritual ceremony for that matter. A "casual" practitioner cleanses by clearing the mind and having full focus on the event. Let us consider a realistic scenario. If an Indian villager who lives in a mud hut has little water to bathe in, returns from a hard day's work in the field just in time to perform agnihotra, does agnihotra with devotion, and it brings healing to the village, then perhaps that demonstrates that bathing is not essential. Bathing is nice if you can do so, but not required for the ceremony to bring results. Most people's days are filled with other essential daily practices and responsibilities. If I had to bathe immediately before each daily agnihotra ceremony, I could not do the ceremony. When possible I brush my teeth and splash water on my face to freshen my mind. After lighting the fire and preparing the rice offering, waiting for the right time to begin the chant, I silently sit and clear my mind. As a usual practice, I do bathe before a special spiritual event as a way to release the energy of where I have been that day and to dedicate myself to the ceremony.

Do I need to wear white clothes while performing agnihotra?

No. It is true that colors have specific vibrational energy and you will find many fire keepers prefer to wear white while performing. On a daily basis, many of us do it in jeans and a T-shirt. Many times I have been working in the garden, stopped to perform, then continued my gardening. I can assure you that I do not wear white when I garden! Usually I wear old worn clothes that I wouldn't even wear to the grocery store. For special events, I do often wear white or other light colors, but this is a personal preference, not a requirement.

I found an Ayurvedic article on the internet that said that agnihotra should be performed to cleanse the atmosphere and prevent bird and swine flu! What do you think?

I agree! How great that you found the article and congratulations on your enthusiasm to seek more information and deepen your understanding. Because I know the potency of agnihotra's effects, I don't worry about pandemics. I follow common sense practices such as sneezing into my sleeve, washing my hands frequently and keeping my immune system healthy. Simultaneously I do agnihotra and encourage others to do it also in their homes. Remember that agnihotra ash and ceremony also neutralize radioactivity. So I joke that in a public emergency I will smear agnihotra ash all over myself and my family, and do the ceremony to protect our community. A student once commented that in doing so, I'll appear so weird to everyone, no one will come near me and that in itself will protect me from disease!

Does agnihotra perform miracles?

It has been said that a miracle is simply a shift in perception. I believe that events referred to as miracles are the way we are all meant to live; we have unfortunately strayed so far from a life of harmony, we become confused and so accept unbalanced living as normal. Rather than consider agnihotra a miracle, I consider it a scientific practice that achieves predictable results, a belief that is echoed by one of my fire teachers. When a miracle can be repeated, as in a scientific experiment, it is no longer defined as a miracle, but becomes an expected outcome from a repeatable process. Such is agnihotra.

When agnihotra becomes a common practice in everyday life, it will be considered natural again and no longer a miracle. That will be a glorious day for us all.

Is this a cult?

Is anything that is a scientifically proven practice, which heals and promotes world peace, a cult? It is only perceived as a cult by those who are uncomfortable with anything of other cultural origins. As you practice, others will observe that you are not losing yourself but instead are becoming more stable within yourself.

A woman I taught enthusiastically began her practice only to have her husband accuse her of being in a cult, and stomping out of the house. She quietly and patiently continued her practice and in a few weeks' time he began to sit down to join her because he realized it helped him feel peaceful.

What can I tell people when they ask what I am doing?

First of all, do not shove it in their face and expect them to embrace it. Don't be like the new vegetarian I sat with at a luncheon who, when someone asked her why she didn't eat meat, responded brashly, "I wouldn't think of eating flesh!", and then after the meal complained all the way out to our car that the people at the table were offended by her being vegetarian. A simple "I prefer to not eat meat for spiritual reasons (or health or ecological reasons)" would have sufficed. In a like manner, you can speak of fire ceremony in terms the other person is comfortable with. "I do an East Indian fire ceremony with cow dung and Sanskrit chants" is weird and far out to most people! "I do a fire ceremony at sunrise and sunset, praying for world harmony and peace" has proven suitable to people who query me. Who can argue with that?

Perform agnihotra to nourish and nurture nature. A Painted Lady butterfly dines on flowers blooming on our agnihotra-healed apricot tree. Photo by friend, Dooley.

It has been my experience that the purity of agnihotra provides a protective zone. People seem to either not notice it, or to accept it without question. People seldom ask what fuel I use or what type of prayer I offer. They assume the fuel is sticks of wood and prayer is English. Those who do ask are usually interested in the process in which case I explain that I use dried cow dung for fuel and sing a prayer in Sanskrit. I explain that while all spoken words contain within them the energy of the meaning of the word, Sanskrit is intentionally focused and potent in its vibrational sound effects, and cow dung is anti-bacterial and aromatic. Which it is! Numerous times when burning agnihotra fire on my balcony, people walking by have said to a friend, "Do you smell something burning? It smells wonderful!"

I have meditated for years and sometimes shared a hotel room with colleagues while traveling on business trips. I arose early to meditate in a chair or sitting on the floor, first explaining to my roommate that I spend quiet time with God every morning. Often they responded "That's a great idea" and joined me! My explanations of fire ceremony are similarly accepted.

What will my friends and family think?

Many will think you have finally gone totally bonkers! Try to not judge them; be gracious and allow them to not understand. It is easier to practice something everyone around you supports. It is more challenging to practice when they think it is meaningless, or worse, harmful. Offer your family the same information that convinced you. If they think smoke will bother them, practice alone outdoors and invite them to smell how this smoke is different. As they begin to observe benefits, they often adjust their thinking. My family accepts that I do this; it simply confirms to them that my life has taken another strange turn. We grew up on a farm and shoveled dung out of the barn, frequently hurling it at each other. My older brother in particular was quite skilled at finding cow patties that were dry and hard on the outside yet still wet on the inside, delightfully splattering upon impact. Little did I realize the precious commodity we were so blithely tossing around!

I am a Christian (Muslim, Jewish, Buddhist, Pagan…). Won't this conflict with my faith?

Why would it? This is a scientific practice. Just as prayer is universally acknowledged, so are fire ceremony, meditation, and compassion to others. Persons who resist such a beneficial practice as sacrilegious, or a practice of darkness, are ill informed and ignorant of a truth. It is not our place to judge them, but to recognize that they have a different point of view. At a spiritual retreat I attended, when the teacher spoke of meditation, a member of the audience said, "This makes sense to me, but I am afraid it is wrong to practice because it is considered bad in my faith. I cannot do it." To which the teacher replied, "If you had been raised Hindu in India, you would believe meditation is essential. If raised Muslim, you would face Mecca to bow in reverent prayer thrice daily. If you were raised Native American, perhaps you would perform the Sun Dance. It is the culture you were raised in that taught you your beliefs. Now that you are an adult, you are free, indeed encouraged, to open your mind to your own universal understanding and to let go of old culturally formed beliefs. What do you feel in your heart to be true? What benefits are gained from your practice? If you are inclined to meditate, then meditate." If you are inclined to perform agnihotra, then perform agnihotra.

I've always been told one has to be a priest of the Brahmin caste from India to perform sacred fire ceremonies.

As with all practices, you will find those who sincerely believe in and teach a "perfect" event. At the other end of the spectrum you find those who are quite casual in how they participate. Most of us are somewhere in between. For centuries, agnihotra was only performed by a male Brahmin priest in a temple after he first received years of training. This was then changed to allow one male to do it in each household. In subsequent times, women were permitted to perform fire ceremony, but not during menses, and only one person was to perform it in any given household. Now some teachers say that the more people that do it in any household, the better. Why has this changed through the years? This is due to cultural changes and expanded awareness taking place among humanity. The essential practice of the actual agnihotra fire ceremony (the science of it) has not changed; only the cultural environment within which it is practiced has changed. It is not our place to judge another by their beliefs. It is, however, our responsibility and joy as an individual to review circumstances and allow the intuitive divine wisdom within us to unfold our personal guidance. Practice with joy and devotion in your heart and your practice can bring transformation to you and all those in your community.

Can I do this on public land?

Yes, providing it is in an area where it will not be a fire hazard. Park authorities will insist it only be done where fires are approved, such as camping sites. While this fire does not normally send out sparks, there are still areas with severe drought where the slightest spark blown out of the pyramid by a capricious breeze could set off a brush fire. In a dry area, such a small brush fire can lead to a forest fire. Take this seriously! Having said that, I have done it in the wilderness with the following precautions: find a large clear spot with no nearby brush, have a bottle of water ready to pour on any unexpected sparks, and a blanket ready to smother any accidental fire. A friend of mine did agnihotra on a large, flat boulder in a state park, in a responsible manner, but it was not an approved area. A passing hiker saw this and called the fire department and they sent out two fire engines!

Can I do this with a group of fire keepers?

Yes! While some people are more reserved, preferring to do it alone, others are enthused to join up with friends. Single fires or multiple fires are both wonderful to offer.

Can children participate or perform agnihotra?

Children love to participate. So long as they are responsible to handle fire safely and to follow the required guidelines, they may do so under adult supervision. I have taught agnihotra to ten and twelve year olds who performed it perfectly. Our granddaughter has attended my daily agnihotra ceremonies since she was a toddler. She sings along, helps prepare dung, and can sit reasonably quiet. I arise early to perform sunrise agnihotra, and occasionally she has chastised me for not waking her up to join me! On

Multiple fire keepers at an evening havan

auspicious dates when I offer one to two hour long fire chants, she sometimes brings a pillow and blanket to lie down and snuggle up by me as I chant and tend the fire. At our longer events, parents bring toys for their children who play quietly as the chanting proceeds. Of course if a child is restless, distracting or noisy, they need to be removed so as to not interfere with the required quiet.

Can more than one person perform this in a household?

Yes. The more who perform it, the more likely at least one practitioner is available at each sunrise or sunset.

How do I know this really works? Has it been proven?

Yes it has been scientifically proven. Even something as subtle as prayer is now proven to bring beneficial effects. Vedic science that has been tested with scientific experiments has proven valid. You can read scientific studies on the websites listed in "Resources". The evidence is clear; it works. You can also read testimonial stories of people who have performed or attended agnihotra ceremonies. A word of caution: as with all practices, some people may claim miracles that are merely coincidence; or that are self-expectation projected onto the event. The results they experience may also be true. Quantum physics demonstrates that the intention of the performer affects the results of an event. Use discernment when learning about any new and unfamiliar practice. Observe your own practice to know if it works in your life.

Do I have to believe in it for it to work?

No. It works according to scientific principles. In time you will recognize benefits and begin to believe.

How do I observe the results?

If you are not yet skilled in the practice of "observing" you may not know what to look for! Possibilities are endless. Here are only a few suggestions to consider:

1. What happens differently than it did previously? A few examples, but not the only ones, are that plants grow larger leaves, colors are more vivid, birds sing with a more melodious sound or more frequently, more birds visit your yard, your senses are sharpened, more people seek you out to spend time with you, and you and your household feel an increased sense of well-being.

2. What do other people remark about? Do they begin to comment on how peaceful your home or yard is? Do they say that they feel better after visiting your space? Are they reticent to leave?

3. Do you feel calmer? Less distracted or influenced by outer circumstances? Are you more equanimous in your thinking and response to situations? Are you more creative? Do you feel lighter or more liberated?

4. What new behaviors are you demonstrating? Did you used to crave sweets but now find yourself wanting vegetables or other healthy foods? Are old habitual patterns shifting? Are addictions losing their "hold" on you?

Are there other Vedic fire ceremonies, what is their purpose, and can I learn them?

There are hundreds if not thousands of havans. They are performed to heal specific illnesses, burned with special woods and herbs, and offered with various chants. They can cleanse an area, motivate, calm, energize, open the mind, open the heart, heal grief, remove obstacles, and provide numerous additional benefits. Of particular note for our planet today is the practice of homa farming, utilizing various fire ceremonies throughout the day and in specific locations on the land. This is proven to enrich the soil, neutralize toxins, promote plant immunity from diseases and pests, and produce abundant harvest. Anyone seriously working with agriculture is advised to learn this practice. Simple agnihotra provides similar benefits to a home garden or orchard, while enriching the entire neighborhood. The list of beneficial havans is long and diverse. Some, such as agnihotra, can be performed in only 20-30 minutes. Others are multiple weeks of duration, and preceded by weeks of special diet and purification rites on the part of the fire keeper. Agnihotra is a most simple and profound havan.

Yes, I teach a few additional havan ceremonies. Websites listed in the "Resources" section of this book also give further information. A word of wisdom from my fire teachers: learn and practice agnihotra first, establishing yourself in the practice and developing a relationship with the fire. With regular and consistent practice, the potency of your ceremony is strengthened. Once you are deeply established in the practice of agnihotra, then you are ready and "powered up" to learn additional ceremonies. I find this to be profound guidance. It is our nature in the West to rush into "more, bigger, faster" practice, causing overload, burnout, and mental indigestion. Simplicity holds potency.

Consider a woman who begins jogging and enjoys the experience. In the beginning she jogs a mile a day, returns home refreshed, showers, sits down to a warm bowl of oatmeal for breakfast and drives happily off to work. She is feeling better, her attitude is up, and she is delighted with this new practice. So she decides it will be doubly refreshing to jog two miles. Now she needs to get up earlier in the morning and gulp down her oatmeal. Then one morning she sees someone else jogging faster which causes her to feel miserably inept. So she purchases a stopwatch to time herself so she can jog a little faster every week. On days she doesn't increase her speed she is disgruntled and goes to work frustrated. Next she hears about a wonderful powder to add to her morning drink for increased oxygenation of her blood. So now instead of having oatmeal she enjoys, she stirs powder into milk. In two months she is jogging further and faster, getting up earlier than she wants, eating a breakfast she doesn't enjoy, and feeling inferior. All because she wanted "more, bigger, faster". Hopefully she will drop all added demands she self-created and return to simply jogging one mile a day, smelling freshly mowed grass, watching birds soar, smiling inside, tasting her warm oatmeal, and driving to work relaxed and ready for the day. Keep your agnihotra practice simple as it is intended to be!

You frequently mention meditation. How does it relate to agnihotra?

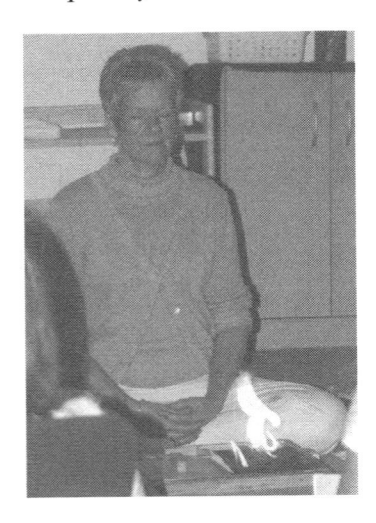

Agnihotra creates an environment that calms the mind, preparing you for a deeper meditation. Together they create a mutually supportive expansion of consciousness. Meditation is as essential to me as breathing. It is my connection with the Source that nourishes my spirit, mind and body. It helps me tune-in to my strengths, dissolve obstacles, and resolve weaknesses. Our children can speak first hand of its benefits. When they were small, if I was grouchy or impatient with them, they would pipe up, "Mom, you need to go meditate right now!" They were absolutely right. Refer to the "Meditation" chapter in this book for an introduction to this practice.

Meditating during a havan

Do you teach agnihotra or meditation?

Yes. I teach agnihotra and meditation. I lead fire ceremonies and offer extended meditations for groups. If you are interested in a ceremony, meditation immersion, or spiritual mentoring, you may contact me via my website at www.CosmicGathering.com. Personal spiritual mentoring and intuitive readings are available by phone or Skype. Contact me to discuss possibilities before a commitment is made.

Both adults and children enjoy learning agnihotra.

When and how can I teach this to others?

I encourage you to teach this once you have sufficient experience to have earned the right. Listen to your own integrity. Never teach it to fuel your ego's need for recognition. Qualities of a teacher and suggestions are included in the chapter, "How to Teach Fire Ceremony".

Final Questions You May Hesitate to Ask

Will agnihotra resolve my life problems? Will that, in itself, expand my consciousness and resolve the planetary dilemma?

> Of course not. Nor will meditation, doing tai chi, chanting a sacred prayer for three hours a day, going daily to confession, visualizing world peace, or giving money to the poor. While any of these may help, they will bear no fruit unless we purposefully and conscientiously practice harmonious living in our daily choices. Since we chose to live in this lifetime, why not make the most of it by living to the best of our knowledge and ability? Why muck around in a murky "comfort zone" of habitual thinking and acting, when we can intentionally choose to act from what actually works? By intentionally applying harmonious living practices with others and the environment, we move toward expanded consciousness. This requires that we intentionally act and respond with preferred behaviors such as patience, sharing with others, encouragement, gratitude, non-gossip, and responsible use of natural resources, instead of reacting with anger, judgment, defensive, selfish, and irresponsible behaviors. We are the energy we express and the positive action we take, and not the knowledge or theories we may have memorized. As one Buddhist monk admonished, "To know and not to do, is really not to know."

Why does the strike plate on a match box wear off before I use up even half of the matches?

> Good question! I run into the same problem and have no good answer.

I tire of being responsible all of the time. Frankly, getting up for agnihotra some mornings is just too much to face. If I miss doing it, is that a sure fire way to ruin my spiritual aspirations?

> Let us "get real" here. Do it when you can and don't feel guilty when you don't. I am confident that you will not "burn in a realm of eternal fire purification ceremony" if you sleep in occasionally.

> There are spiritually evolved beings who don't do fire ceremony. Having said that, it can be a real boost to your spiritual confidence to commit to such a spiritual practice. I find results of regular practice to be worth the extra effort. A little mental trick I play on myself is to say, "Okay, girl, if you are really tired, when you complete agnihotra you can go back to bed." I never do. By the time the fire burns out, I am vitalized and refreshed, ready to go. If that doesn't work, there is always coffee!

I bought a fire kit. It just sits there. My initial enthusiasm ran out. What do I do now?

> Attend another fire ceremony to get "all fired up". If that doesn't work, go online to read of the amazing benefits. If that doesn't work, contact me for a pep talk. If that doesn't work, keep lugging that kit around each time you move. If you initially connected with it, chances are in the future when the timing is right, you will reconnect. Many people do.

I have this uncontrollable urge to add additional items to my fire. Herbs. Spices. Seeds. What is going on?

> Are you someone who tends to overcomplicate things, and then burn out? Keep it simple! (Oh, I think I may have said that elsewhere in the book...). Or perhaps you have a cosmic memory of performing more complicated fire ceremonies and feel "called" to pick that up again in this lifetime? If so, contact one of the resources online for guidance on more complex ceremonies. I list several in the "Resources" chapter of this book.

Why do some fire ceremony practitioners act so serious, as if they are going to be sent to the principal's office if they do something wrong or if they appear to enjoy themselves?

> I think this is very sad. I, too, have seen people look overly stern, or strike a dramatic pose as if they are playing a grand role onstage. I personally find that it is a joyful experience to offer a meditation, prayer, or ceremony! I've observed that Mother Nature, animals and plants have a wonderful sense of humor. It is true that one may appear solemn as they learn because they are so focused. However once one becomes adept, I love to see them perform with genuine love glowing on their face, or a smile on their lips and a twinkle in their eye. Wholeness is all about being joyful!

Do I really have to go through all this "stuff" to be enlightened?

> No. Absolutely not! You can wake up each day, know you are an individual expression of something divine, live your life in harmony with others, be responsible, experience joy, keep it simple, and live a fulfilling life. Wonderful! If, however, you struggle to remain established in such a realized state of being, havan and meditation are only two of the many tools that can support you and help you support others.

- Notes -

Chapter 6

Personal Agnihotra Experiences

When I began this book I did not intend to share personal stories of agnihotra benefits, thinking it best to limit it to practical advice. Yet when I teach agnihotra, it is the stories that inspire and bring hope. I am no different than the rest of you in this regard; the stories motivate me to pursue knowledge! When I mentioned preparing this book to my students and friends, without exception everyone proclaimed, 'Include the stories!'" I share here only a few of many experiences I've enjoyed. Within them, perhaps you will find an invitation to bring transformation into your own life.

Woodpecker Finds Renewal

In Chapter 2, I shared an incident where Ron and I cleared the environment of a rental house we were cleaning for our daughter. The morning after our "clear out the cat smell" experience, we performed agnihotra in the living room and then drove to a restaurant for breakfast. We slowed down for a flock of large woodpeckers on the street, but one didn't fly off and the car hit it. We stopped to check on it and it appeared dead in my hands, with its tongue hanging out; blood dripping from its mouth and from a cut on its right leg, and a limp left foot. Yet its heart was still beating wildly. So we returned to the house to meditate by the still-warm agnihotra pyramid, with Ron holding the woodpecker in his hands. It lay totally limp with its head resting on Ron's wrist. He sprinkled cooled agnihotra ash on the bird's back, gently stroking it into the feathers. Its heartbeat and breathing slowed down. This was surprising, because a bird's heartbeat is naturally rapid, and a wild bird is usually frantic when captured. This one rested quietly in Ron's hands for fifteen to twenty minutes as we meditated. It then opened its eyes, continuing to rest quietly in his hands. Moments later it pulled its tongue back into its mouth, continuing to rest. Eventually it stirred, stood up and flew up to perch on a piece of wood decor near the ceiling, landing on its two feet which now appeared normal. It rested there for several minutes. We opened the front door, and it gracefully flew directly outside to land on a tree branch near the front window. It perched there for three hours, with its head tucked under its wing as it rested, then it stirred and flew off. Our daughter reported that for the following several weeks a beautiful large woodpecker occasionally sat in that tree for a few hours each day and then never returned. While we recognize the bird may have initially only been stunned, it also regained use of its left leg, its right leg stopped bleeding, the blood disappeared from its mouth, and most interesting, it totally surrendered into Ron's care. We intuited that agnihotra was at work here.

Toxic Smells Diffused

After the morning agnihotra and bird incident, bad smells remained absent in the house. During the day we continued to clean. Usually when we use strong cleansers, such as chlorine bleach, the fumes cause a toxic reaction in me and I get headaches, achy muscles and sore lymph nodes. I worked with chlorine and other strong cleaners all day in the house with no side effects. I literally couldn't smell fumes! Our daughter similarly reacts to fumes and she noticed the same benefits. It is as if agnihotra had totally dissolved all toxins from the house's environment. They used paint stripper on the cabinets - normally I would have to leave - this time we couldn't smell it! The real test for me on whether something is toxic is that the day after exposure I experience flu-like symptoms of sensitive skin, chills, fever, headaches and deep fatigue as my body strives to clear out the toxins. The day after this experience I felt great. This was in itself a miracle to me that could not be explained except to consider agnihotra fire had indeed cleared toxicity from the atmosphere of the house.

Regular Daily Practice Changes Our Plants

To test the benefits of agnihotra to my own satisfaction, I committed to perform it for every sunrise and sunset from September 1999 to January 2000, and then continued to practice regularly several times a week over following months.

Every fall after my chrysanthemums, lantana and other flowers died back, I always moved the pots out behind our backyard shed where the plants would freeze and die over winter and I could re-use the soil and pots the next spring. When I went out to use them the following spring, vigorous green growth was emerging from among old dry stems. The only water they had received was from irregular snowfall, yet they were still alive. I placed them back into the sunshine, watered them, and watched as they put forth new blooms with larger flowers than the prior autumn. After Ron put agnihotra ash on them, one of the chrysanthemum plants that had deep maroon flowers began to offer blooms of peach coloring on the same plant. While I know that putting ash or other additives on soil of plants can change the color of blooms, I've never seen two colors of blooms on one individual plant.

By our front entrance I planted a red impatiens plant. When purchased it was full of blooms. As those blossoms died, no new buds emerged. I began sprinkling agnihotra ash around on the soil and scattered it over the plant as well. New leaves emerged which were large and lush, fully fifty percent larger than before, and emerging buds bloomed equally larger than the original blooms.

The prior summer our cottonwood tree had borers causing a large branch to die. We planned to cut it off in the spring. Over winter I put ash on the trunk and around the borer holes. Next spring there was no sign of borers and the "dead" branch fully leafed out again with no signs of damage. Our local nursery owner said this was not possible, but it happened.

That fall one of our silver leaf maples was sickly. Its leaves were slightly curled, smaller in size than our other silver leaf maples and it appeared to be dying. I rubbed ash on its trunk and sprinkled ash around its root area. The following spring its branches filled out again with lush leaves and a dove nested in its green branches.

We also had a large patch of St. Augustine grass in our front yard with severe grub damage. It was yellow and dying; most was totally dead. I could pull up handfuls of grass because the roots were entirely eaten away. The next spring we planned to replace the dead area with new grass. I left the dead grass over winter to protect the soil. One January day I decided to experiment by spreading a half cup of agnihotra ash over the dead area to see if it made any difference. At least melting snowfall would soak the ash into the soil so that grass we planted the next summer could benefit. I then forgot I had done this. One spring day our youngest daughter ran into the house exclaiming, "Mom, come see the front grass!" New grass shoots were emerging, including in the "dead" area! There was no dead spot. When we examined the grass, it had grown new roots and it greened up as if it had never had damage. I asked the owner of our local plant nursery if grass killed by grubs could grow new roots over the winter and he emphatically said no!

Our five-year-old Aloe Vera plant bloomed a tall lush purple bloom that spring. It had never bloomed before; I didn't know it could!

New Birdsong

The spring of 2000 we had a greater variety of birds, and they sang more. We never heard so much singing! A grackle moved in to a tree outside our bedroom window. I remember thinking, "Oh no! I thought agnihotra was supposed to improve the environment but it has just caused me a problem". Grackles offer a raucous call that many consider undesirable, including me! Yet over spring and summer of that year its call softened and it emitted a new sweet chirp I've never heard them make. A neighbor heard it and asked what sort of bird made that noise and didn't believe it was a grackle until I pointed it out in the tree.

Other than the St Augustine grass' miraculous comeback, which I know was impossible; the other events cannot be directly proven to be the result of agnihotra. Yet with my many prior years of gardening and animal care, all these events appeared to be out of the ordinary. They indicated that some life force and energy was at work that was out of the normal. The only difference we could trace it to was agnihotra.

Agnihotra in an Apartment and Condominium

In 2000, we moved from Texas to New Mexico, where we lived in an apartment for several years, subsequently moving into a new condominium. Due to my work schedule and other commitments, for five years there were months, especially in winter, when I performed agnihotra less frequently, maybe only twenty times a month. I performed it on our second floor balcony in both locations. I do not know what kind of tree was planted outside our condominium, but it grew significantly faster than other trees of the same type in our condo community. During these years I also taught agnihotra to a significant number of people, many of whom began to tell me their own amazing stories of benefits they received.

New Home for a Combined Family

Since I first began the practice, agnihotra continued to offer unusual events in our lives and lives of others who practiced it. In August 2006, we enthusiastically decided to combine into a three-generational home with one of our daughters, her

Agnihotra chimineas for my daughter and me. Our resident mouse frequently observed ceremony from under the rosebush.

husband, and our 12 month old granddaughter. This house had a small yard where I could regularly perform agnihotra and my rapidly increasing repertoire of fire ceremonies.

Our yard soil was poor, yet with regular agnihotra it subsequently grew lush plants with abundant vegetables. Without fertilizer, and only due to the agnihotra environment and ash sprinkled at its base, a spindly five-foot-tall apple tree with four limp limbs developed into a strong, beautiful, spreading twelve-foot specimen in only one year. A sickly, aphid-infested rose bush healed and began producing ongoing fragrant blooms from March until frost. Where I performed agnihotra on our back patio, plants grew toward the agnihotra pyramid, leaning forward to catch the fragrant smoke and hug the air. When flowers in patio pots had a choice to grow toward the sun or toward the agnihotra pyramid area, they preferred the agnihotra.

Our granddaughter began to sit by the agnihotra fire, chanting along. Sometimes when I performed the fire, a little mouse scuttled out from its home under our nearby air conditioner, peering cautiously from behind a flower pot, or seated under the rosebush. Slowly developing trust, it ventured nearer. One day it scurried over to hide behind my foot, watching the entire ceremony as it peeked around my toes. Soon it bravely sat to nibble ghee off the outside of my ghee jar placed only six inches from my knee. Birds sat on stucco walls of our courtyard and occasionally flocks landed on the edge of the roof above my head to sit as the fire burned. A pigeon couple built a nest and raised a fledgling on the parapet directly above my agnihotra location, cooing us awake in the mornings. I might add that no bird droppings landed on the fire area, which may be the most amazing story of all!

This house was located near the Albuquerque petroglyphs. These are natural cliffs from an ancient lava flow which holds carvings of ancient pueblo people of the Southwest. Since our move to Albuquerque this particular area had held a mesmerizing attraction to me. Now I lived there and as I walked the hills, they felt familiar to me as if I were returning to complete something that had remained unfinished. As I conducted fire ceremony there, I felt I was assisting with something greater than myself. This led me to visionary experiences which I will share another time, perhaps in another book. Because of this when we decided to move from there to a new home two years later, I felt conflicted. The move would be beneficial for all of us; closer to our work, to a house with a bigger yard, closer to the community of friends we had established. Yet I sensed my fire ceremonies were needed where we currently lived and I didn't want to leave until my service there was complete.

On a Saturday morning just prior to our move, I asked the Divine to give me an answer to my dilemma. Was my work there completed? Had I accomplished what I had been sent there to do? I began an extended fire ceremony which I usually chant for one to two hours. As I chanted, a flock of blackbirds swirled and landed on the eaves above my location, cawing along with my chant. I wondered if this was my answer. They flew off only to be replaced by a group of turtle doves that swooped in to sit on the eaves, cooing loudly. Surprised, I felt my heart begin to release responsibility I had held for two years. The doves flew off. Then on the nearby courtyard wall, a group of tiny red-headed finches arrived from where they lived in succulent plants of our neighbor's yard. They chirped and hopped atop the wall, their song joined by sudden loud chirping of sparrows in nearby hedges. By now, tears were streaming down my cheeks as the thought crossed my mind, "Where are the orioles?" The song of orioles has always touched me deeply in a way I do not understand and some lived in a neighbor's tree across the street. At that exact moment, a flock of orioles flew over my head. My chant continued as sobs arose from my heart and I knew I had accomplished what I had come to do. I could now leave. My fires, in some unknown way, had served. In this place I had moved more deeply into the potency of fire ceremony. I had transformed into a new level of Being that would go with me to new locations, to serve in new ways.

New Home, New Opportunities

We moved to a home with a larger yard, offering our granddaughter a secure place to play, with trees to climb and space for a larger garden. As usual, natural miracles happened. As a young girl growing up on the Kansas prairie, one of my favorite wild flowers was known as "Snow-on-the-Mountain". This wild plant is a lovely dusty green with leaves outlined in brilliant white. While it blooms with small white flowers, its true beauty is in the showy leaves. After college, I married and eventually we moved to Texas. On a visit home to my father's Kansas farm, I mentioned how I loved "Snow-on-the-Mountain" plants and wished I had some for my Texas garden. He promptly got up from his chair, grabbed a spade from the back porch, and headed across the dirt road to our cattle pasture. There he dug up three plants, placed them in old coffee cans and turned them over to me. Carefully I packed them into my car along with our two daughters and luggage to drive us back home. There we lovingly planted and nurtured the plants in a corner garden where their roots took hold, allowing them to fully expand into large showy plants which delighted me to no end! One evening I returned home from work only to discover that our landscaping company had killed all my "weeds" including my wild "Snow-on-the-Mountain"! I was deeply wounded by this travesty but eventually forgot it as I moved on with my life.

Snow-on-the-Mountain wildflowers

Now, thirty years later, we returned to our agnihotra-supported yard from a three week trip and I settled in to perform evening agnihotra. As I chanted the mantra, there in front of my eyes was revealed a fully blooming "Snow on the Mountain" plant! With closer observation I discovered two more in the same garden. They had not been evident when I watered there three weeks earlier. Somehow they had moved in and made themselves at home. I had planted no seeds, had not thought of this wildflower in years, and yet here they were. I researched online and learned it does not normally grow wild in our area of New Mexico. I do not know how it arrived in my garden, but you cannot blame me if I believe that nature appreciated my sacred fires, and bestowed a gift of appreciation in return!

Pine Cone Gift

I now practice my daily havan at a brick fire place I built in a protected corner of our back yard. The pyramid sits within three brick walls, covered by a tile roof. This protects the fire from wind and rain. When performing havan, I remove the tile cover so fire can reach and dance far up into the air, replacing the tile cover once the fire burns out. Occasionally I forget to replace the cover, leaving it open during the day. On such occasions, the ash has always remained protected in the pot, even during strong winds. One evening when I went out to perform sunset agnihotra, I discovered I had neglected to re-cover the fireplace, and found a new discovery. The ash had all disappeared. Perhaps it had blown out, although that had not happened before. As an added surprise, a small pine cone had neatly dropped into the precise center of the pyramid. Something had "used the ash" and given me a "gift" in appreciation. Yes, perhaps a frisky wind blew out the ash, and another frisky gust blew in the pine cone. You may believe what you wish. As for me, I again thanked Mother Nature for our ongoing joyful, cooperative friendship.

Christmas Tree Starts a New Life

One of my fellow agnihotra practitioners and her husband watered their Christmas tree with agnihotra ash water. They noticed that the tree needles remained flexible and green during the weeks leading up to the holiday. Following Christmas, when they went to remove the tree from its stand, they discovered new roots growing out from the cut trunk! They celebrated by committing to plant it outdoors in the soil the following spring. That tree deserved a new chance at life!

New Herb Appears

Summer of 2011 I began writing a book on nutritional and healing benefits of local, edible wild plants. As I wondered through our herb garden, making notes of wild plants we use, I felt overpowering appreciation and love for the many domesticated and wild herbs we enjoy in our gardens. Mint, lemon balm, lavender, rosemary, oregano, chives, sage, roses, Vitex, mullein, Echinacea, and mallow.

One day I noticed a new plant growing next to our mullein. Not wanting to weed out something significant, I let it remain to see how it developed. Eventually it set out lovely small daisy-like blooms, but I still did not know what it was. I found a second

Feverfew "surprise" in herb garden

plant blooming, hidden by the cat mint plant in another garden. A friend thought it was chamomile, but further research indicated not. Then I accidently came upon a picture of feverfew and that was it! How did feverfew arrive in our gardens? By now, you know what I suspect – the mystery side effects of agnihotra's cooperative relationship with nature. A new herb arrived in our garden to teach me its story. All is contained within the quantum field.

Gatherings

At this agnihotra-blessed home, new and experienced fire keepers practiced together, offering multiple fire ceremonies for benefit of the community, metropolitan area, and the Southwest. Other fire keepers in our area also teach agnihotra and hold fire ceremonies. What we do here connects with healing ceremonies offered by other traditions, whether fire, prayer, dance, singing, chanting, or other forms. Together we heal each other and the planet.

I practice agnihotra as frequently as possible with my daily schedule. Accumulated benefits are evidenced daily. I teach this practice to anyone who requests to learn, as others graciously once taught it to me. I now offer additional fire ceremonies, yet agnihotra is the foundation, the cornerstone, that which nurtures the potency of the other fires.

A gathering of fire keepers

When writing this book I was stumped with a computer program formatting problem. I looked at it from various angles but could find no answer. As I sat before my sunrise agnihotra fire one spring morning, an obvious solution popped into my head and it proved perfect. This is a common occurrence with both fire ceremony and meditation. Solutions are readily available to life's mysteries when we sit in the silence and tune in to the infinite wisdom within.

Final Thoughts

No one of my experiences can be proven to be the result of agnihotra. Yet the accumulation of these frequent experiences is not common to the world at large. Something unique is taking place. I was raised on a 300 acre farm of rolling hills on the Kansas prairie where we raised cattle, sheep, guineas, pigs, and chickens. We planted a garden to feed a family of six, and grew acres of wheat, oats, barley, alfalfa, sorghum, milo, sedan grass, and field clover. As a child I roamed these fields and spent hours reading in treetops while birds hopped and perched nearby. I eagerly pedaled my big brother's beat-up red bicycle up and down the hilly dirt roads, listened to the song of coyotes playing under the moon, rescued injured rabbits and birds, ran with

Our Agnihotra garden in the high desert in July 2009

our dogs and cats through the pasture, and sang to the sunset when it was so beautiful my heart felt it would burst. In those years I merged with Mother Nature and we became dearest of friends. I know Nature.

Agnihotra is a gift to her, offering an energy force she can transform into the necessary energy forms to heal. I do not require confirming scientific experiments; I only need to tune into the heart of our planet to know the truth.

Agnihotra heals.

- Notes -

Chapter 7

Agnihotra Ash Remedies

Does agnihotra ash heal? According to personal testimonies, ancient Vedic writings, and some recent scientific studies, the answer is a resounding "yes!" As with all suggested healing solutions, please use it with discernment, observing its effects for yourself! Do not apply any recommended healing remedy blindly. I find it heals as well as some natural or herbal remedies and perhaps better than others. At the same time, some experiences others relate of their use of ash do not work for me. I believe in it sufficiently to apply it frequently with successful results. Your personal experience provides your own verification.

These are suggestions, not promises. I created many of these remedies early-on by adapting recipes from other alternative and herbal concoctions I use. More recently, pharmacist Monika Koch has written a wonderful booklet with agnihotra ash remedies, which is listed in the "Resources" chapter. I am not responsible for any results you experience; you are personally accountable for applying these remedies in your life. Some of these are supported by scientific studies; others are not. If something doesn't sound right to you, don't try it. Refer to the websites listed in "Resources" for additional healing remedy publications and verifying scientific studies.

Making Ash

Place ash resulting from the fire into a kitchen strainer set over a bowl and stir it with a spoon until the fine ash falls through. This fine ash is what is collected and used for healing. The ash "chunks" remaining in the strainer can be added to plants or soil.

Storage

Store ash and ash potions in lidded glass, ceramic or copper containers. Ash can be stored in paper as well. Do not use plastic or metal. This ash does not lose its potency even if stored for years.

Ash Application

Ash can be used directly on wounds, rashes, on plants, or mixed in with soil. Ash applied directly to skin may cause light stains as it rubs off on clothing or furniture fabric, so you may want to cover the application with a band-aid or cloth. Some of the following remedies stain the skin or clothing; others are used without staining. Use your common sense.

Ash Condiment

Fill a salt shaker or recycled spice shaker with strained ash. Keep on your table with salt and pepper shakers, and one by the stove. Shake onto food at the table, or add to soups and sauces. This especially goes well in tomato sauce dishes such as spaghetti, pizza, salsa and chili. It offers a slightly smoky flavor.

Ash Water

- Mix 3 rounded tablespoons of sifted ash with one gallon of purified water in a glass jug. Less ash is alright if you are short of ash.
- Shake and let sit in the sun for 3 days.
- Strain resulting water through a cloth placed in a strainer. (Ash sludge remaining in the strainer can be added to soil.)
- Drink the water, spray on plants, put one cup in bath water, use for various healing remedies that use water, replacing regular water with ash water.

You can store ash water in a clean glass jar or jug for a long time; agnihotra ash is purported to keep water from turning bad. I've stored it for as long as six months, without using the boiling process mentioned below, and when opening the jar, the water smells and tastes as sweet as the day I bottled it. Only once did I open a bottle and it smelled funny so I immediately threw it out. I never determined the cause. For greater safety for long term storage, wash empty juice bottles in the dishwasher on the hottest cycle possible, or sterilize with boiling water. Wash the vacuum bottle lids and drop into boiling water and turn off. Then bring the ash water to a boil. Pour boiling ash water into the pre-washed glass juice bottles and screw on the lid. Gently invert to heat and sterilize the lid for five minutes. Turn upright and place on a towel. As jars cool, the lid seals and locks air out of the bottle. Label the jar with the date on a piece of tape and store on shelves in dark area or in a cabinet. The air-tight seal and beneficial ash maintains purity for long term use. As with all canned and stored items, if you open it and it does not smell fresh with a subtle ash smell, but instead smells strange, discard it immediately. You can access research on this topic online.

Ash water sitting in sunshine

Google "agnihotra ash water crystals" to find an online photo of an ash water crystal as developed by Dr. Masurao Emoto's renowned technique of photographing crystals of healthy and unhealthy water.

Quick Ash Salve

This salve is quick to make and easy to use. Yield: 8 ounces salve.

- Add 1/4 cup sifted ash to 1 cup ghee.
- Bring to a boil, lower to a slow simmer and simmer for 1 to 2 hours.
- Pour the hot ash ghee through a cloth placed in a strainer over a glass or stainless steel bowl. BE VERY CAREFUL; HOT GHEE ACCIDENTALLY SPILLED ON SKIN CAN CAUSE A SEVERE BURN.
- Pour strained ash-ghee into small glass jars. Add lids and place on a towel to cool. Store.
- Resulting salve may appear grainy; it isn't. These are "bubbles" of moisture and dissolve instantly as you rub it onto your skin.

Apply to wounds, sores, rashes, sunburn. This can also be taken internally. This quick salve could leave a slight brown stain if left on fabric, but I've never had this happen in my experience. Of course any oil can leave a slight stain if not treated.

To moisturize skin: Mix a little salve in your palm with your moisturizer or lotion before applying.

Ash Decoction Salve

Why decoct? A decoction is only slightly more complicated yet forms a more potent remedy. This salve is amazingly emollient, fragrant, and does not stain.

Yield: 16 ounces of salve.

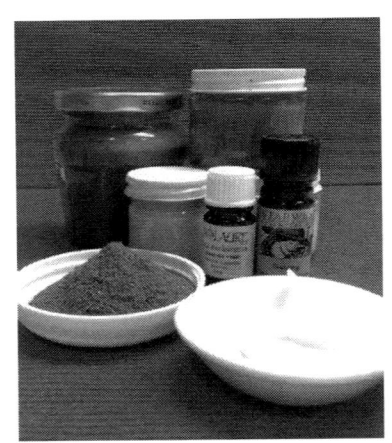

- Add 1 cup sifted ash to 8 cups water. Bring to a boil, lower fire to a low simmer. Cook down to one fourth of the original amount (i.e. cook 8 cups water down to 2 cups).
- Pour the hot ash water through a cloth placed in a strainer over a glass or stainless steel bowl.
- Cook the resulting 2 cups strained ash-water with 2 cups ghee at a low simmer until the water cooks out (approximately 4-6 hours). You know the water is cooked out if you toss in a few drops of water and it sizzles.
- Pour decocted ash ghee into small glass jars. Add lids and place on a towel to complete cooling. Store.
- If desired, stir in a few drops of essential oils to the slightly cooled solution. Some of my favorite essential oils are lavender, rose, sandalwood and tea tree. Go online to learn the benefits of the various essential oils. Examples: rose and lavender promote healthy skin, sandalwood and rose are cooling, and lavender and nutmeg promote sleep.

Sifted ash, quick ash salve (dark jar), decocted ash salve (ivory), lavender and nutmeg essential oils

Apply the salve to wounds, sores, rashes, sunburn. This can be taken internally if essential oils are not added.

To moisturize skin: Mix a little salve in your palm with your moisturizer or lotion before applying. Or use on its own. This decoction does not leave a color stain.

Ash Massage Oil

Yield: 24 ounces

- Pour one cup each of coconut, sunflower and sesame oil into a quart jar (or use any single or combination of oils desired, such as almond or jojoba).
- Add 4-6 tablespoons sifted ash. Stir or shake well.
- Cover with lid and let sit in sun for 7 days. Shake daily if desired, but this is not necessary. Ash settles to the bottom of the jar and the oil becomes smoky-colored.
- Pour oil slowly through a cloth placed in a strainer over a glass or stainless steel bowl.
- Store the resulting strained oil in a glass jar.

Use for massage as needed. It also can be swished in the mouth for 2 minutes and rubbed on cleaned teeth and gums at bedtime, or add a small amount in with lotion to apply after a bath.

Ash for Plants

Use ash on indoor plants, gardens, landscaping or agricultural crops.

Rub ash on leaves, stems, and trunks of wounded, damaged or infested plants.

Scatter on soil around plants and trees, and then water it into the soil. Ash serves as soil enhancer. It stimulates microbe activity in soil and improves water retention.

Dust ash onto infected foliage.

Spray ash water onto infested or infected foliage. Spray on mites or aphids. *It is not poisonous* but causes them to disperse. It will not harm bees, butterflies or birds. When sprayed at sunrise or sunset, leaf pores are more expanded to receive healing energy of the water.

Animals

Use ash with animals in the same way as for people. You can sprinkle ash on areas infected by fungus, mites, or other unwelcome tiny critters. For an outdoor pet, rub ash gently into their fur and sprinkle it into their sleeping area. If applied to indoor pets, this unfortunately carries unwanted ash residue into other areas of the home. So, after bathing a pet, pour (strained) ash water over the fur and rub in. Sneak ash into your pet's food and water. Rub ointment on distressed areas. They may like to lick ash-ghee salve off your finger or hand.

Environment

Add ash to water: rivers, fountains, tanks, ponds, lakes or any small or large body of water. I put ash water into the birdbath to help heal wild birds. I never put ash alone directly into the birdbath water as I am concerned the ash particles could become lodged in the birds' tiny respiratory tract.

Summary

I only list here a few of the many uses which utilize ash and ash water. As you journey online to the resource websites, you will learn amazing information. I encourage you to be creative in your application, trusting your intuition to lead you to new uses in your own life. As I continue to do agnihotra and work with the resulting ash, I feel connected with the fires in a very personal way. Insights come to me; I experiment, observe and deepen my understanding.

- Notes -

Chapter 8

Ghee Preparation

Ghee is clarified butter, meaning impurities have been removed. Making it yourself is reasonably easy to do, but not everyone has time to undertake "one more" project. It is wonderful to make your own. If you cannot, you can purchase at most health and natural food stores. Many additional instructions are available online.

Ingredient -: One pound of *unsalted* butter (four sticks)

Yield - approximately 1.5 cups ghee

Utensils

- One medium saucepan (avoid aluminum or Teflon coated)
- Spatula
- Fine mesh strainer or regular strainer with 3-4 layers of clean cheesecloth or similar material.
- Clean a glass jar and lid. (I pour boiling water into mine, invert and let sit a few minutes to disinfect the lid, then drain and thoroughly dry before use).

Procedure

- Heat unsalted butter in a non-aluminum sauce pan over medium heat setting.
- Allow butter to melt, bring to a boil, stirring constantly.
- The oil will separate into layers.
- Skim off the frothy layer on the top.
- Once the oil has become clear, remove pan from heat.
- Allow to cool 15 minutes.
- Pour cooled ghee into the prepared jar through the strainer and/or cloth. This strains out the residue from the bottom of the pan.
- Secure lid and store on shelf in cool dark location.
- Ghee stores indefinitely. Avoid dipping into it with a wet utensil. Mold does not grow in this purified ghee, but it will grow around any foreign liquid or food introduced into the jar by "double dipping". If this happens, scoop out the moldy area with a clean spoon. The remaining ghee is fine. Good ghee smells neutral, sweet, or nutty. If for any reason it smells sour or rancid (rare), discard it.
- Ghee does not need refrigerated but can be if desired. It will become hard.

- It is said that ghee which is 10 years old or older is excellent medicine. Ghee stored for a long time becomes whiter and somewhat translucent.
- The color and flavor of ghee can change slightly according to what the cow was eating when the original milk was obtained for the butter.
- Ghee has no milk solids, so can be heated to a higher temperature than butter or most oils without smoking or burning.
- You may find information stating that ghee and clarified butter are not the same. This is usually explained by the differing methods of making it. The recipe listed above is quicker to make and fine for cooking and using for fire ceremonies.

Alternate Slow Cook Method

Follow the instructions above. When the froth covers the surface, gently reduce the heat to the lowest setting. Simmer uncovered without stirring for 45 minutes, or until the milk solids on the bottom of the pan turn golden brown and the butter on top is transparent. Strain the ghee and store as above. This method imparts a unique nutty flavor to the ghee. Please go online for any necessary additional instructions for making ghee or for information on the many health benefits and possible contraindications (rare) for using ghee internally.

- Notes -

Chapter 9

Dung Preparation

Dung used for agnihotra must be from a cow. Not from a water buffalo, horse, goat, donkey, sheep, turkey, chicken, cat, dog or other non-cow animal! (Another tradition may use dung from other animals as part of their ceremonies. I am told that some African tribes use elephant dung in spiritual ceremonies.)

Source

The cow may be of either gender and of any age. Ideally you want it from cattle raised on an organic farm, freely grazing on pastureland. Preferably the cows are not treated with antibiotics, fed animal byproducts, treated with growth hormones, fed genetically modified food, or living in an unsanitary feed lot. Next best is finding happy cows grazing on pastureland. The top option is if the farmer actually knows the cows' names, pats and scratches them occasionally and tells them jokes. Find a friendly farmer who won't mind you wandering purposefully among her cows, gathering freshly dropped dung.

Gathering

Carry a plastic bucket or container and wear rubber gloves. Walk the pastureland scooping the fresh dung into your bucket. Do your best to not gather up sticks, rocks, or extra grass that is beneath the dung. If you will carry this inside your car for a long distance, may I suggest you use a container with a tight fitting lid? Dried dung is fragrant. Fresh dung is described differently.

Preparing

At home, lay out a sheet of plastic on a sufficiently large flat surface such as a concrete patio, picnic table, plywood or other surface. Scoop out the fresh dung, smoothing it out onto this surface in a large rectangle, patting it down to ¼ inch in depth. Then with a spatula, knife, or pizza cutter, gently "score" it half way through into 2" x 2" sections or the desired size of dung pieces. You want the dung pieces to fit into the copper pyramid. You can always break these pieces into smaller sections if needed. After a while you will know what size works best for you. I have seen many variations including pieces that are 1"x4" and 1"x2".

Allow the dung to dry thoroughly. Resulting dung texture, color and fragrance varies according to what the cow was eating. Break dried dung into pieces along the scored lines. You can be more imaginative in your drying techniques. You may make flat "dung patties" separated by spaces so they thoroughly dry out. One woman slaps wet dung onto the outside walls of her farm silo (a large cylindrical building which stores cattle feed), then peels it off when dry. I have a fun image of dung slapped onto the top of a car which dries as one drives around doing daily errands or to and from work. It certainly would make an interesting conversation starter! I suppose that could also be a form of protection if a nuclear explosion happens nearby while driving!

Storage

Store dried dung in a paper sack, cardboard box, wooden crate, or straw basket. Do not store in plastic or metal (except for copper or gold). Store this in a waterproof location. I store mine in cardboard boxes which stack neatly in my backyard shed.

Additional instructions are found online. See "Resources" in this book for ordering dried dung. This is how most practitioners procure their supply. Practice harmonious thinking, and pay the requested fee requested with a good attitude. My heartfelt appreciation goes to the devoted practitioners who gather and dry the dung for the rest of us to purchase. This is a time consuming and dedicated task.

- Notes -

Chapter 10

Build a Simple Outdoor Havan Fireplace

I created a raised fireplace out of materials I had laying around the back yard and it works beautifully. You may have other leftover materials lying around to assemble your own unique creation. I recommend creating a raised fireplace such as this one so that the fire pyramid is at a convenient level as you perform the ceremony. Unless it is raining or snowing, I remove the top tile, allowing the flame to rise up and burn freely. Once the fire burns out, I replace this tile to protect from possible moisture until I burn the next fire.

A fire in my completed outdoor fireplace

Supplies

I used various sizes of tiles and bricks in the photo. However, the supplies I list here are standardized and will be easier to use, but *will not exactly match up with the photo*. Adopt and adapt to use what you have on hand or what you can find.

- 32 standard bricks
- 1-18"x18" one-inch thick square pavestone (16"x16" is shown in the photo)
- 2-18"x18" ceramic tiles

Assembly

- Determine a flat area where you will build your fireplace.
- Measure an 18"x18" area where you will place it.
- Foundation: Stack 12 bricks on the floor. Using six bricks, arrange two stacks of three bricks each, end to end along the right side of your area, aligning the outside of the stacks with the edge of the area. Repeat with six bricks on the left side.
- Place the 18"x18" pavestone on top. This serves as the floor of your fireplace, located up high for ease of access and to place your fire pyramid up near your body's fire center. I also placed an 18"x18" ceramic tile directly on top of the pavestone to add a smoother surface which is easy to wipe clean. The copper fire pyramid will be placed on this tile floor.

- Fire kit area: Stack 19 bricks on top of the pavestone. Arrange so the outside walls are four bricks high. The back wall is three bricks high to create an opening for smoke to flow out the back.
- Note that the walls in the two back sections are slightly inset so that the three back bricks are neatly centered between them.
- Place the second 18"x18" ceramic tile on top of these bricks. This is the top of the fireplace. Smoke exits out the opening in the back. On clear days I slide the top tile forward to create a larger opening in the back for the smoke to exit, or as mentioned earlier, remove it entirely to allow the fire and smoke to move freely out the open top. The extra brick can be inserted into the back smoke hole on windy days or for extra protection and removed when doing the ceremony.
- As you perform, the fire is well protected from the wind, rain and snow.
- Note: Bricks and tile are not cemented together. It is not necessary, and this allows you to move your fireplace to other locations.

Assembling the structure

The pyramid is well protected inside the fireplace on a snowy day. Notice the two red clay pots that hold and protect the agnihotra supplies.

Chapter 11

Resources

Most of these resources offer services at cost or for minimal profit. They devote their lives to promoting and supporting sustainable living and sacred fire ceremony for the benefit of the planet and all humankind. I deeply appreciate each for their respectful and committed service. We depend upon them for supplies and information and they never fail to serve.

Required Supplies: (See "How to Practice the Ceremony" for details.)

- Copper pyramid of specific proportions
- Stand for pyramid
- Copper spoon
- Copper lid for pyramid*
- Copper tongs (optional but recommended)*
- Copper mixing bowl (optional)*
- Organic brown basmati rice (white rice may be used but brown is preferred)

- Organic ghee (clarified butter)
- Cow dung (preferably from an organic farm)
- Wooden matches
- Morning and evening agnihotra mantra
- Sunrise/Sunset time chart for your zip code area
- Clock that registers seconds accurately (A small handheld satellite clock is highly recommended.)

These supplies are not required. However a serious fire keeper will eventually use them.

Information, Supplies, and Equipment

You will find a multitude of agnihotra resources online. In alphabetical order, I first list the two websites I utilize. Both offer equipment, supplies, time charts, video demonstrations, audio recordings and cassettes/CDs of the agnihotra mantras and more. Information is correct as of this printing.

- Website: http://www.agnihotra.org
  Email: info@agnihotra.org; Phone: 540-407-0273
  This organization provide teachings as led by Vasant Paranjpe, disciple of Shree Gajanan Maharaj. Paranjpe made his transition in 2008 and his devotees continue to steadfastly support his work. Learn about agnihotra farming practices, referred to as homa farming. Read experiences of agnihotra practitioners from around the world in "Satsang", their bi-monthly

publication. Richard hand-makes and sells high quality copper equipment and travel kits at his own copper works. See his catalogue at www.agnihotrasupplies.com

- Website: http://www.agnihotrausa.net
  Email: Yogini at agnihotrausa@yahoo.com
  They provide teachings as led by Mohan Jadhav, disciple of Shree Gajanan Maharaj. Mohanji's warm hearted wisdom and teachings continually radiate out onto our planet. Here you can listen to the recordings of many mantras for ease of learning.
- Ellie Hadsall, Albuquerque, NM: CosmicGathering@gmail.com
  (for supportive information, encouragement, and to schedule ceremony and training only please. See the above resources for supplies and equipment.)

Scientific Studies

Most websites listed here include valid scientific studies on agnihotra and its effects.

Homa Farming

Many websites included here refer to homa farming. Tapovan center in India has practiced homa farming for years, website: www.tapovan.net.

Online sites

- A video primarily demonstrating the use of agnihotra: http://www.homatherapy.org/content/om-shree-dham-homa-farm
- Homa farming results - http://www.homatherapyindia.com/category/image-galleries/homa-farming-results

Sunrise/Sunset Time Charts

You need a sunrise/sunset time chart for your zip code area. There are several different methods of time calculations and you need the *specific* method used for this purpose (local weather, TV and radio station times are not correct for this purpose).

- Time charts are available from the websites listed here.
- If you have a smart phone you can download an Agnihotra app, "Agnihotra, or iAgnihotra" from Vedic Society. It's convenient, specific to your location and ideal for travel. It includes an alarm.
- *Always check your time chart to assure it is adjusted for the daylight savings time change in your time zone. If not, you need to adjust it yourself.*

Websites

www.agnihotra.org; www.agnihotrausa.net/; www.tapovan.net; www.homatherapy.org; www.homatherapyindia.com; www.agnihotraindia.com; www.terapiahoma.com; and more!

Agnihotra Ash Healing Therapy

"Homa Therapy – the Ancient Science of Healing", by Monika Koch, is readily available if Googled online. It is a well presented booklet explaining the use of ash for medicinal and healing purposes. A pharmacist, she set out to experiment with the healing ash and she created recipes. How I wish I had this book when I first began!

Dung ("Gomay")

- Many websites listed above offer dung.
- Prof. Sankar Sastri, Pennsylvania: Lakshmi Cow Sanctuary, 610-599-8824 or 610-653-7079, email sankar1@yahoo.com Sankar saves cows from the slaughterhouse; this is the cows' dung; funds help provide for the cows. Meet the cows at www.cowprotection.com.

Ghee

Ghee is available at most natural and health food stores.

Small Atomic Clock that Counts Seconds

- Radio Shack and Office Depot have offered them in the past.
- http://www.mfjenterprises.com/Product.php?productid=MFJ-133RC offers one.

To Learn Agnihotra

This book is a good starting point, or added support if you are learning from another teacher. If you have a group of individuals seeking to learn agnihotra or meditation, contact Ellie Hadsall at CosmicGathering@gmail.com. Also see listed websites; several teach it online or will refer you to a teacher near you.

Writings on Agnihotra, Homa Farming and Other Planet-friendly Practices

Secrets of the Soil: New Age Solutions for Restoring our Planet, by Peter Tompkins and Christopher Bird, Harper and Row, New York, 1989. This book is filled with stories of pioneers who early on led the way to true soil health and balance. Included is a chapter on Agnihotra.

Meditation

Center for Spiritual Awareness, Roy Eugene Davis, Director.
http://www.csa-davis.org   Phone: 706-782-4723
Roy Eugene Davis is a direct disciple of Paramahansa Yogananda. His enlightened, clear and practical guidance has changed countless lives, including mine, propelling us forward into the experience of the Divine. His teachings guide my spiritual practices and offerings. His center offers regular spiritual retreats and quality support. Additional meditation resources can be found online. Note: I am writing a comprehensive, encouraging and realistic book on meditation, "Meditate on This", that will be available soon - check Amazon, or my website.

Ayurveda

The Ayurvedic Institute, Vasant Lad, BAMS, MASc, Director
11311 Menaul Blvd. NE, Albuquerque, NM 87112
https://www.ayurveda.com/   Phone: 505-291-9698
Ayurveda (Life-Science) is mentioned throughout this book, and is a Vedic sister science to Yagnya/Havan/Homa and Hatha Yoga. A natural lifestyle and holistic healing practice, it offers practical, clear and insightful guidelines for health, vitality and longevity. Many health food and natural products stores now carry Ayurvedic products and herbal remedies. Contact the Institute for authentic, quality education, books, information, and products. Additional Ayurvedic resources can be found online.

- Notes -

Chapter 12

How to Teach Agnihotra Fire Ceremony

All aware beings on the planet can now consciously co-create our future. Fire ceremony, as with meditation, is a foundational practice upon which we can build a harmonious existence for all life forms.

Are You Ready to Teach?

You earn the right to teach when you have gained experience through personal practice and you are established in agnihotra as a regular part of your life. It is not necessary to have prior teaching experience or formal training. If you pray, and you experience the power of prayer, do you need certification to teach your child or a friend how to pray? Not if your heart is clear and you earned the right through your own life experience. Agnihotra is the same. As you practice intentionally and consistently, you will know without a doubt that this ceremony shifts the energy and heals. With this understanding, and your own application, you are divinely prepared to share it with others.

Qualities of a Teacher

A good teacher demonstrates the following characteristics:

1. Humility

   This is first and foremost. If you teach with humility, your students feel safe to listen and ask questions. They believe that they, too, can practice this. If you teach to gain notoriety or power, you are not teaching; you are taking advantage of another's trust for your own personal gain. Unfortunately for both you and your prospective students, this is not "good" karma!

2. Sincerity

   Speak and demonstrate with a genuine desire to assist others. Be honest with your students about what you can and cannot do. If you do not know the answer to a question, admit it immediately and seek the correct answer. In this way you encourage your students to ask questions fearlessly, and you deepen your own practice.

3. Earn the Right Through Personal Experience

You cannot teach until you are ready. Teaching from information in book, or another person's experiences, does not impart quality teaching. When you have regularly practiced fire ceremony, made mistakes and corrected them, observed results in your own life, and are filled with enthusiasm, then is the time to teach to others. This may happen within 30 days or 3 years. Time is not a factor! I began sharing my fire ceremony experience with friends within two months of my first ceremony. I talked about what I knew, frequently needed to acknowledge what I did not know, and together we sought answers from experienced outside resources. Some of those friends taught others and many are still practicing 12 years later.

Teaching agnihotra

However, as a reality check, let me share with you my experience of teaching meditation. In the 1980's my husband Ron and I attended a highly respected spiritual center for a week of spiritual guidance and meditation. We both already meditated twice daily on a regular basis and had done so for 15 years. We certainly had observed the many benefits of meditation practice. During this event, the spiritual teacher encouraged all who were present to establish meditation centers when they returned home so that others might also learn. During a lunch break, a fellow participant enthusiastically shared with us how she was going to immediately start a meditation group in her city. She appeared genuinely motivated, yet we observed she was highly reactive to outer events, judgmental in her conversation about other attendees and life, and pushed constantly for her own agenda. We recognized there could likewise be qualities within ourselves that precluded us being ready to teach.

Upon our return home, I committed to that Divine Intelligence, which has always guided me, that I would only teach meditation when others began to approach me to learn. I would seek to continue practicing spiritual principles, allow my personal experiences to develop deeper understanding, and when appropriate, let others know I meditated. When the universe determined I was ready to teach, it was responsible for sending me my students. Until then, I was not ready. I assumed it would happen fairly soon. Yet it was three years later when finally one of my business clients asked me if I would teach him how to meditate. The next week, a friend asked me the same question. Two weeks later I received a phone call from the minister of a regional church asking me to substitute teach a class about spiritual principles because the regular teacher had to leave town for a family emergency. In that class, students asked me how to meditate, which I heartily agreed to teach. I thanked the universe for its confidence in me, and began my many years of teaching meditation.

4. Respect other teachers.

Everyone who teaches brings their own experience and life viewpoint into their offerings, including me. This leads to variations in style and technique. As is frequently mentioned in this book, there are foundational concepts which are essential for a fire ceremony to be agnihotra. Yet within each tradition of teaching, there are added practices or rituals which that group deems important and valuable. It behooves each of us to respect these variations while at the same time adhering to our own innate path of expression. Vedic philosophy teaches that each of us is unique as we proceed toward healing and self-liberation. Any pathway that leads to harmonious living and expansion of personal understanding is valid.

My primary mode of operation is meditation and contemplation to connect with my divine source and to establish myself in that nature, and then to bring the resulting understandings into practical practice in everyday living.

I find many of my students are intelligent, sincere beings who are never-the-less insecure within themselves, having been conditioned by their upbringing and social interactions to not trust themselves. Instead, they feel it is safer to follow guidelines set down by another person they deem more important or wiser than themselves. Yet those same people come to me quietly and hesitantly to ask questions of how to express those spiritual teachings realistically in their daily circumstances. While I am happy to assist, if you are one of these, I suggest it is time for you to begin trusting your own innate knowledge, that direct truth which seeks to flow into your conscious awareness. It is time to cease blocking it out or not trusting it. Now is the time to be the "master of your soul", to recognize and trust the intuitive part of yourself that observes and comprehends without need for outside verification. This is a new and incomprehensible way of living for many, yet the time has arrived on our planet to shift to this inner trust.

Organize

Now that you feel prepared to teach, you are ready to organize your thoughts, equipment and supplies. Refer to this book for ideas and suggestions.

- Plan the steps of your presentation in the order in which you practice.

- Review your equipment and supplies. Be sure all is ready for your demonstration. Rehearse how you will demonstrate and build your sample fire.

- A helpful way is to conduct a sunrise or sunset ceremony, sit in silence to meditate for 10-20 minutes, and then teach. If sunrise is too early or sunset too late for teaching, you can do a sample agnihotra process, explaining that it is not the "real " event, but even so is a wonderful meditative experience.

- For each key step of your presentation, offer examples, stories, studies or other references to add credibility and make it more memorable in the participant's mind.

- As you share, acknowledge your own mistakes, offering them as valuable learning experiences so that your students are not discouraged by their inevitable mishaps, but instead encouraged to learn from them. Some wholesome humility is a wonderful gift!

- Anticipate the questions you may receive. What questions did you have when you were learning? Include the answers in your presentation. Review "Frequently Asked Questions" in this book for ideas. By being prepared, when questions are asked you can respond clearly and concisely. Plan time for questions and answers at the end of your talk.

- Rehearse your talk to assure it fits within the promised time frame of your presentation. Remember that any presentation takes more time than anticipated. Be sure to leave at least ten minutes for questions and answers at the end of the program.

- Prepare handouts for participants to take home, or refer them to resources. For free PDF handouts that you can download and copy to share, contact me at CosmicGathering@gmail.com.
- If your fire demonstration does not run smoothly, such as the fire is difficult to start, or it burns out before chanting time, use this as an opportunity to confirm these things happen in real life. Encourage the participants to not be discouraged or judgmental, but instead to learn from such events. And remember that it is not outer circumstances that cause us discomfort, but rather the way in which we choose to participate with them. Remain centered, humble, and express a good sense of humor. In this way you demonstrate that you are centered, gracious, and confident. Which, of course, you are!

- Notes -

Chapter 13

Simple Meditation Guidelines

If you decide to learn meditation, or are merely curious, this chapter serves as a simple introduction. If you are ready in mind and spirit to proceed, this basic information begins your practice. The procedures need not be complex, nor do you need to be initiated by an "enlightened" spiritual teacher to benefit from meditation. Many regular meditators picked up a book, practiced, and were able to proceed with multiple benefits. My husband taught himself from an early hatha yoga book and was an experienced meditator long before meditation arrived into current western social awareness.

If you are not merely interested for mental entertainment, but truly yearn to meditate for the purposes of superconscious transformation, contact me for support. I have meditated daily since 1972 and taught it since 1990. As an ordained minister in the Kriya Yoga spiritual tradition, it is a joyful and inherent part of my life. I credit it with keeping me connected with the greater Divine Field from which I receive consistent guidance and assurance. Currently I am writing a comprehensive and realistic guidebook on meditation, "Meditate on This". It will include numerous meditation techniques, as there are myriad ways to apply this universal practice. As with agnihotra, meditation practice raises questions best answered by a qualified teacher.

Meditation is simple and benefits are profound.

I've learned from multiple sources, yet the most profound, deep, and clear teachings came from Roy Eugene Davis, a direct disciple of Paramahansa Yogananda. His contact information is included in "Resources" chapter of this book. You can find additional information online.

Why Meditate?

Do you "know" you are more than this lifetime, yet don't know what that might be?

Do you experience an empty void in your life and yearn to fill it up with something but cannot find what that is?

Do you believe in something greater, beyond current experience, and want to connect?

Do you seek to be established in your connection with the Source, however you perceive it to be?

Are you wound up so tightly that you don't remember what it was like to truly relax?

Are you worn down by life challenges and seeking a refuge of solace and healing?

Is your mind constantly chattering and probing, and you'd like mental peace and quiet?

Do you feel separated from unconditional love?

Would you enjoy more mental clarity? Emotional stability? To open your heart?

Meditation is a simple, natural process which benefits you on all levels: body, mind and spirit. You remain conscious, alert and inwardly peaceful. Body and mind are rested and healed. As thoughts quiet down and the mind becomes calm, you become increasingly aware of your true nature which is in command of mental attitudes, states of consciousness, mental processes, feelings, and behaviors. In essence, meditation is the cessation of all mental activity, leaving a quiet mind that can observe and receive intuitive information.

Preparation

- Choose a quiet, undisturbed time and place.
- Keep the room dimly lit or dark.
- Commit to the experience, deferring other activities until meditation is complete.
  Turn the sound off on your phone, don't answer the door, and tell family or roommates to not interrupt you.
- If possible, meditate at the same time daily.
- Sit in a firm chair or on the floor in a comfortable position where you can remain erect.
- Many people find meditating in the morning upon arising before engaging in the day's activities is helpful or in the evening as you settle down for bedtime.
- Avoid food or stimulating drink for one hour prior to meditation.

Simple Steps for Meditation

1. Sit comfortably upright, with spine straight but not stiff.
2. Relax. Gently breathe deeply a few times to assist the process. Begin to breathe naturally, observing your breath, gradually smoothing it out.
3. With inhaling and exhaling, focus your thought effortlessly on a chosen word-sound or phrase, such as "calm", "peace" "om" or even the word "one". You want to think of this word, but not speak it out loud.
4. When you become aware your mind has wandered away from focusing on the word-sound, as it naturally does, let go of that wandering thought, and gently bring your attention back to "listening" to your focus word or sound.
5. Continue as long as comfortable. Then when you feel centered or inclined to do so, release your word-thought to sit in the calmness. Seek to sit in this meditative situation, from start to finish, at least 10 minutes, extending gradually to 20-30 minutes.
6. Conclude, coming out gradually by again observing your breath and body, opening your eyes when you feel re-oriented to the room. Never rush out of meditation. You are often deeper than you realize, even when your mind seems to have constantly wandered!

Results

Results are cumulative. Consistency of practice is essential to experience benefits. Do not look for "exciting" experiences or "amazing" visions. That is indicative of a searching, grasping mind from which you seek to release. Do not say, "That meditation was worthless because my mind constantly wandered to other thoughts." You will still have experienced subtle benefits. Simply follow the process regularly with no attachment to results. In time you experience benefits including a calmer centeredness during the day, less emotional reaction to events, more creativity, and a more focused mind. See additional benefits listed at the end of this chapter.

Helpful Suggestions

Do not fight your mind as if it were an enemy! I relate with my mind and body as two dear assistants that I created to support me through this life's experiences. As I love them, they serve me well. I trained my mind to function as it does; now I respectfully ask it to assist me in this meditation endeavor by forming new patterns of quiet so we both can rest and find Divine refreshment. My body likewise assists me. For years, I and my two assistants have benefitted by regularly diving deeply into this sanctuary!

Do not judge your meditation experience. Sit down, do your best, and let results unfold naturally. Even "busy mind" meditations are beneficial. The key is to be sincere and committed to practice, with intent to quiet the mind by focus on your word-sound.

Do not compare meditation experiences with others. If you have questions or concerns, discuss them with a qualified teacher who can give you clear guidance based on your own unique situations. Everyone's experiences are different, depending upon their practices and personal growth patterns. Experiences of phenomena, or lack thereof, are not a measure of your level of meditation success.

Measure results of your meditation by observing changes in your outer, daily life. When you and your actions become more centered and beneficial, relationships become more meaningful and supportive - then you know your meditation is indeed progressing.

Benefits of Meditation

- Stress reduction
- Mental and emotional clarity
- Clears conditioned mental patterns
- Increases creativity
- Enhances positive outlook on life
- Slowing of biological aging processes
- Deepens relaxation, reaching the cellular level
- Allows more orderly thinking
- Improves intellectual ability
- Strengthens the immune system
- Promotes healing
- Enhanced sense of peacefulness
- Expands spiritual awareness
- Deepens attunement with your inner self and wholeness
- Heightens intuition
- Diffuses and releases addictions
- Creates even-mindedness in all circumstances
- Minimizes dependence upon outer events and people to bring you self-fulfillment

What Superconscious Meditation Does Not Include

- Hypnosis
- Mind programming
- Reverie
- Sleep
- Dreaming
- Loss of consciousness, or coma
- Astral travel
- Channeling
- Opening you to negative forces beyond your control
- Psychic experiences
- Visualization or affirmations

- Notes -

Chapter 14

My Journey to Healing Fire Ceremony

My connection with fire ceremony was a total surprise! This is ongoing evidence to me that if we are to connect with something or someone, the Divine will bring that connection about. We only need to be "available and willing" to participate! After regular agnihotra practice for four years, during a meditation in 2003 I was guided to write this handbook. What began as a small instructional handout during my training seminars expanded into what you hold in your hands today.

Since my earliest memories, my life has been intimately connected with a Divine presence. I was raised in the Christian tradition with parents who sought to apply Christ-like principles in their lives, each according to her/his nature. In my personal experience, my parents were surprisingly open-minded in their understanding of the principles and this encouraged me to trust in my own understandings rather than blindly accept beliefs of traditional society in which I lived. My mother prayed daily, and clearly stated to me on more than one occasion that Christ was special, yet in other cultures there were similarly divinely inspired persons who trod on Earth, demonstrating and teaching principles of love and compassion, and each brought hope to the people of their land and generation. My father, a college educated agricultural agent, said he did not need to go to church on Sunday mornings because the quiet house when all of us were gone, and his daily time spent as a farmer outdoors with the land, plants and animals, was his communion with God.

As youngest of four siblings, who was of course teased whenever possible, I kept my dear connection with the Divine a closely guarded secret, yet it was deeply interwoven into my consciousness. I learned to quietly make choices, and often took action, only after first measuring it against my ever-expanding spiritual understanding. When I acted in harmony, I felt strong inside. When acting contrary to my "knowing", I inevitably regretted it. In time, I came to prefer the feeling and sensation of acting in harmony.

It has been an up and down journey to apply the spiritual truths into my daily life. It has taken trial and error to get the hang of how to apply them into life on this planet! Yet over the years those same truths have expanded me into magnificent new realities. And woven through my life's fabric there has been a special thread that always pulls me back to an inner "knowing" that we are more, we are important, we are supported, and each of us is unconditionally loved by an unseen Divine source.

When the Beatles musical group re-introduced meditation into awareness of Western world, my husband, Ron, and I learned a transcendental meditation technique. It was perfectly supportive of non-traditional spiritual path we had been forging in our own life. With meditation, I felt even more "plugged in" to that Divine intelligence and regularly experienced clear guidance through intuition. In 1988 we were introduced to Kriya Yoga, a non-denominational spiritual path taught by Paramahansa Yogananda, which resonated deeply with us both. Seeking a living teacher, we found and received profound teaching and support from Yogananda's disciple, Roy Eugene Davis. We practiced teachings of this path with intention, integrating it into our lives, and in 1993 I was ordained in this tradition.

In 1995, I had difficulty sleeping one evening. I slipped out of bed to settle into my favorite chair in the living room where I could read and occasionally stop to gaze out into the starlit Texas sky. I was reading "Mad Bear: Spirit, Healing, and the Sacred in the Life of a Native American Medicine Man", an inspirational and entertaining biography written by Doug Boyd. Over the years I had felt intuitively drawn to Native American life and this book was again reconnecting me with their wisdom and wit. I came upon a chapter describing Mad Bear's attendance at a United Nations event and as I read it I felt a strong message come to me, "You will attend a U.N. peace event." Now this was downright silly, because I lived in the suburbs of Fort Worth, Texas; United Nations was in New York and I was in no way associated with such events. My life certainly did not point in that direction and I had no time or money to pursue it. Yet the message was clear. As I was wont to do, I put it back into the hands of the Divine, saying something akin to, "Well if you think this is to happen you sure do have your work cut out for you, because I just don't see it." And I let it go.

A few months later a student at our spiritual center approached me one Sunday morning with the Dallas Morning News paper. "I don't know why, but I'm supposed to give this to you. This issue. Today." We both chuckled, knowing there was something in that paper for me to read, but due to a busy schedule I set it aside on a table at home and forgot about it. Two weeks later, I sat down one evening, bored, looking for something to read. I glanced at the Dallas newspaper and picked it up, curious to see what it might offer. The religious section included a small paragraph describing a "Multi-Faith Exchange" group that met regularly to share worship experiences of different faiths. This piqued my interest, as my husband Ron and I had often observed how religions had much in common and we wished to honor this commonality. I called the organization to talk with the director. The organization admitted two people representing each faith and each was already represented. He asked, "What is your religion?" When I replied, "Kriya yoga" and explained that, no, it is it not physical yoga stretches, and no, it is not actually a religion, but instead a very practical spiritual path, he eventually concluded it could be added in as a new group. Thus Ron and I joined this integrating organization and began to participate with multiple faiths.

One holy day we attended services at the local Islamic mosque. Following a beautiful service, we sat in their fellowship hall chatting with their people. I overheard a conversation nearby that went something like this: "Yes, being asked by the United Nations to hold this peace conference in Dallas for the world's religious leaders is a real honor. But we are going to need lots of volunteers to assist us." Oh…my…God…did I really hear this right? With a racing heart, I walked over to him as calmly as I could possibly pretend, and offered, "I would love to volunteer at the conference." I was immediately accepted and scheduled to assist. My actual responsibility would be assigned the morning of my volunteering.

A week before the 1996 U.N. gathering in Dallas, the director called me with a question: "We received a fax from the world representative for Kriya Yoga. If I hadn't met you, I would have thought this was a hoax. Is he legitimate?" He spelled out the man's name, which was an ongoing series of Sanskrit titles, names, and credentials. For simplicity, I will refer to him here as "Jagad Guru". We learned he was indeed legitimate. He never publicizes his teachings or promotes an organization. Anyone who is connect with him is "led" to him through personal connections and intuition. I was told that because of his official position in India, he was traditionally expected to never leave the soil of India but this would be an exception, due to the peace initiative of this event. Oh…my…God…did I really hear this right? With luck perhaps I would actually see this holy man who was the designated representative for my spiritual path at this gathering of world religious leaders!

The approximately 200 world religious leaders would meet in small groups of fifteen to twenty delegates each, to discuss and develop suggestions for reaching world peace. I was assigned to sit in one of those groups to record the discussions. At the last minute, I learned the director had graciously assigned me to the group which included the Kriya Yoga saint. Oh…my…God…did I really hear this right? As I headed toward our meeting room, I gave constant thanks to the Divine for this opportunity.

This day held many additionally miraculous moments and deeply meaningful connections for me. I periodically went to the ladies room to look at myself in the mirror to be sure I still existed in physical form, and hadn't died and gone to heaven! During the lunch break I called my husband Ron to check in and confirm that my life outside this experience still existed. In brief summary, I personally met with this Kriya Yoga saint, as well as divinely appointed personal meetings with additional holy women and men of other traditions. This spiritually uplifting experience transformed me in multiple ways that day, and in days to come. The dear divine connections made that day continue to serve me well in these ensuing years.

Among "Jagad Guru's" entourage was a well respected Hindu man from Houston, Texas who invited me to attend a fire ceremony there which was to be held for the purpose of blessing a friend's home. A special event in their lives, this would be to be offered by "Jagad Guru", who subsequently invited me personally to attend. Ron and I promptly accepted and traveled to Houston for the ceremony. This specific havan was quite elaborate with offerings of fruit, various spices and herbs, and continuous chanting for two hours, with the sweat pouring off the swami's head and soaking his saffron silk robes. A transcendent warmth from the fire ceremony descended over me, energy in the room shifted remarkably, and every cell of my body began to sing. Something special was going on here. This felt very *familiar* to me and I wanted to know more.

At that home blessing, I asked this saint, "Who can teach me fire ceremony?" and he responded, "I do not teach this, but you will find someone." Six months later I was invited to speak about the science of meditation at a public conference on Vedic science. Up on stage with me were three scientists speaking on the three Vedic sciences of sound, architecture and fire. The sciences of healing through sound and fire were introduced and I again was prompted to pursue this practice. I asked, "Who can teach me?" and the scientist I asked responded, "I don't teach it but you will find someone." After two more years of searching, I one day had the intuition to again purchase a book I had read and given away eight years before. When I received my ordered copy of "Secrets of the Soil", by Peter Tompkins and Christopher Bird, I therein discovered an entire chapter dedicated to the practice of agnihotra and the science of fire! I hadn't noticed this chapter in my first reading. Divine timing was again at work in my life.

I promptly sought out and phoned the people mentioned in the book. These were pre-internet days, so they sent me a brochure which explained the procedure. I purchased essential equipment and began practicing. I made three phone calls with clarifying questions which they graciously answered.

While I am enthusiastic to learn new practices, I am equally cautious until they are proven to work. So I set out to test agnihotra for myself. I practiced the fires in my home at every sunrise and sunset for four months. Results were so astounding I knew I was onto something major. As I continue the practice it has proven to be transformational for me, my family and community. A few experiences are included in the "Personal Agnihotra Experiences" chapter of this book.

Several teachers have blessed me with their teachings and support. "Jagad Guru" introduced me to sacred fire ceremony and encouraged me to bring the practice into my life. Richard and Lisa Powers of The Fivefold Path in Madison, Virginia, graciously answered my questions and supported me in my first days, providing necessary equipment, supplies, and encouragement. In 2003, Vasant Paranjpe, teacher of Richard and Lisa, traveled to Albuquerque where we lived. He committed his life to teaching fire ceremony to the householder, traveling to teach and establish agnihotra centers around the world. Ron and I were fortunate to host his entourage and him while in Albuquerque. In 2008 I met and received continued teaching and support from Mohan Jadhav, a brother disciple of Paranjpe, who has lived as a householder, experiencing the balance of working and raising family while traveling the world, teaching, leading sacred ceremonies and establishing centers to bring this science into the hands of any sincere seeker. We have been blessed to host him several times in Albuquerque. During my nine-plus years as education administrator at The Ayurvedic Institute, the school's founder, Dr. Vasant Lad, and his staff provided an inviting and supportive environment to offer and teach fire ceremony to students and the community.

During agnihotra ceremony meditations, the fire itself has offered me innumerable and profound insights which guide our mutually co-creative processes and experiences. In addition to these mentioned, I feel it equally important to recognize friends, family, and many students who have encouraged me to pursue and share these cosmic truths. My immediate family has tolerated and encouraged my various endeavors as I have sought to find my way on this unique journey. At the root of it all is the Divine guidance that has always connected me with the right practices, teachers, and resources at the right time.

It is the community of all souls that we exist within that is to be honored here. I include many of my teachers' resources in the "Resources" chapter of this book. They don't teach for personal recognition. They teach because it is their joy and life purpose to do so. My community also includes you who join me by reading this book and trying this out in your own life. So to each of you, I thank you.

Chapter 15

The Next Step

You have information. The next step is to put it into action.

Knowing how to perform fire ceremony does not build the fire nor does mere information heal you or the planet. Now you need to gather equipment, chose a location, set up your ceremony area and arrange your life to begin practice. If you feel inclined to do agnihotra, consider that you are invited to do so by a Divine Intelligence that knows what is needed and that is willing to assist you in unseen and unknown ways.

To help you get started, consider answering the following:

When do you commit to practice? (Weekends? Mornings? Evenings? Three times a week? Once daily?)

Where will you set up your agnihotra space?

What equipment/supplies do you need?

What obstacles do you need to overcome first? (Lack of confidence, how to explain it to others…)

Where can you go for support, encouragement and answers to questions?

Who can you invite to attend your agnihotra fires, and to share this new spiritual practice in your life?

If you feel confident, proceed with no hesitation. Practice, learn, adjust, refine. With experience you will become established in the practice. Then enthusiastically teach others with humility, recognizing you are only the one who performs the action. As Mother Teresa responded when being complimented on her dedication to serving the poor, "God is the writer; I am but the pencil in God's hand".

If you feel guided to do fire ceremony, yet are insecure, uncertain in yourself, or need assistance, contact me or one of the resources I have shared! Share with me your experiences so we can celebrate together!

Email: CosmicGathering@gmail.com

Website: www.CosmicGathering.com

Blog: http://cosmicgathering.wordpress.com/

Agnihotra Shop: http://www.cafepress.com/AgnihotraHavanOnEarthShop
   Here you will find clothing, mugs, aprons, toys, and a wide assortment of agnihotra items! Includes items for adults, children, babies, pets - humorous and traditional.

May your life be filled with blessings,

May you be observant to perceive them,

May you express your gratitude into the world,

May you find joy in small things,

May you intentionally co-create a harmonious existence,

And may you live in the knowledge

That you are unconditionally loved and supported by the Universe.

~ Ellie

Observation Journal

Keep a journal on these pages of the positive results you observe from your agnihotra practice. In this way you verify its benefit, establish yourself in the practice and build confidence to share with others.

Observation Journal

About Ellie Hadsall

Ellie Hadsall is a minister, author, and Vedic fire practitioner. Introduced to transformational Vedic fire ceremony in 1996, first she privately practiced to prove their potency to herself, and then began teaching it to others. Focused on introducing this ancient practice into western culture, she has taught hundreds of students from the United States and across the globe; many are now fire practitioners in their own communities.

She considers herself a work in progress. Her life has been filled with twists and turns that lead her on a wildly imaginative and rewarding journey. She holds life as an assignment to gain insights, expand understanding, and joyfully assist others to forge their own journey.

Her life has included ordination in the Kriya Yoga tradition, creating and directing a spiritual center, teaching truth principles from a variety of respected spiritual traditions, and mentoring clients in personal and spiritual self-development. Currently a spiritual mentor and inspirational speaker, she is avidly devoted to her writing. *Learn more at www.CosmicGathering.com/About*

Books by Ellie

Agnihotra: Havan on Earth
A Simple and Comprehensive Guide to the Practice of Agnihotra,
a Vedic Fire Ceremony for Personal and Planetary Healing

The first and only comprehensive Agnihotra guidebook on the planet. Practical, informational, and entertaining. Includes photos and pages for personal notes. Non-Fiction. Available at www.Amazon.com

Nature's Garden: Edible Wild Plants in a City Yard
Don't weed your yard; munch your way through it!

This downloadable booklet includes how to indentify, harvest, prepare, the nutritional value, traditional healing uses, and delicious recipes - all from weeds! Includes color photos. Non-Fiction. Available at www.CosmicGathering.com

Books Coming Soon!

Pathwalker: A Soul's Journey through Reincarnations
Book 1 of the Cave Time Series

Eleni knows she is a soul, and makes life choices from that perspective - until the day the foundation of her existence is pulled out from under her. Suddenly she must make life and death decisions with no clear guidance. She faces overwhelming hardship, meets unexpected soul friends, and hopes to remember what she has learned as she moves into her next life. Eleni's struggles are our struggles; her victories are our inspiration. Join her for a spiritual adventure of the highest order, one that is sure to influence your life choices! Fiction – a download the author received from "Source". Available at www.Amazon.com

Meditate on This
A Comprehensive and Practical Guide to Meditation for Personal and Spiritual Transformation

Learn the science of meditation and clear instruction on a variety of methods. Appropriate for all religious and spiritual traditions. Non-Fiction

For more information contact Ellie at www.CosmicGathering.com

Made in the USA
Lexington, KY
05 May 2017